THE GEEK'S GUIDE

HOME BUYING

CRANE HILL
PUBLISHERS

ISBN-13: 978-1-57587-254-4
ISBN-10: 1-57587-254-4

Design by Miles G. Parsons

Printed in the United States

Library of Congress Cataloging-in-Publication Data

James, Karen.
    The geek's guide to home buying / by Karen James.
        p. cm.
    1. House buying. 2. Mortgage loans.   I. Title.
    HD1390.5.I85 2006
    643'.12--dc22

2006031073

THE GEEK'S GUIDE

HOME BUYING

Karen James

CRANE HILL
PUBLISHERS

CONTENTS

Buying into the American Dream 7

Deciding to Take the Plunge 9

Preparing for the Purchase 15

Getting to the Core of Your Credit Score 21

Estimating Your Expenses Easily 31

Looking for a Money Tree........................... 39

Getting Approval from Others 45

Applying Yourself................................ 51

This Loan's for You! 61

Homing in on Homing Options..................... 79

Deciding on Your Dwelling 91

Understanding the Role of Agents......................... 97

Signing with an Agent 111

Taking the Grand Tour 119

Let's Make a Deal 129

When the Deal Goes Through 139

Sealing the Deal 155

Geek Glossary.................................. 161

Index 189

BUYING INTO THE AMERICAN DREAM

So you think you want to buy a house? Home ownership is a great way to spend your money, and although some experts don't like to call it an investment, it usually produces good return on your money and years of pleasure and pride.

Deciding to buy a home is one of the biggest decisions you will ever make. Not surprisingly, there are serious questions you should ask yourself before making this decision. The good news is that the more thought you give this ahead of time, the smoother the whole process will be.

The Geek's Guide to Home Buying will help you make the right decision by providing information on every step of the home-buying process. And because there will be critical, but probably unfamiliar, terminology used from start to finish, you'll find a very usable glossary in the back of the book for quick reference. This handy volume can keep your dream from turning into a nightmare by offering an overview of what to expect, and a practical and useful roadmap once you get started.

DECIDING TO TAKE THE PLUNGE

Buying a home is a big step. Really big. It's probably the biggest purchase you'll ever make, so give it lots of thought before you do anything. Let's look at some important considerations you should think about before buying.

First, let's think about reasons most people buy a home. There are some compelling reasons to buy:

- It puts your money (and other people's money) to work for you.

- Interest paid on your mortgage may be tax deductible, which can mean huge savings on your taxes.

- Unlike rent, which disappears each month, your mortgage payment goes toward equity in your home. That's a resource you can tap into later and use to make home improvements, pay off other bills, or to help with unexpected expenses.

GEEK*Speak:*

"Real estate is the best investment in the world because it is the only thing they're not making anymore!"
Will Rogers

GEEKOID

A recent survey indicates that 68 percent of American families own the homes they live in.

- It increases your net worth.

- A more subjective reason is that you have the satisfaction of owning where you live. You can paint the walls any color you choose and then hang pictures on them, complete with nail holes if you want, without checking with anyone.

All those reasons are good enough to make you decide to buy a home. But before you charge ahead just because it sounds like a good idea, here are some other very practical considerations to think through.

On the average, people in the United States move to new homes about every seven years.

- Timing – Be sure now is the right time for you personally to buy a home.

    If you think you'll be going back to school, or if your job might be relocated to another city, now is not the time to buy. But if your family is growing and you want to find a cozy nest for all of you, now might be the right time to act.

    Also with regard to timing, do you have the time needed to look for a home? If you need somewhere immediately, you may be better off renting an apartment that you can move into almost as soon as it is located.

- Needs – While it is tempting and fun to rush out immediately and start to drive around and look at houses, think realistically about what and where would best meet your family's needs.

- Affordability – Most people do not have money on hand to entirely pay for a house. They will need to get a mortgage. But there are some expenses that will have to be paid for up front. Do you have enough money on hand for the down payment, inspections, reports, and closing costs? Is there money in your budget for making monthly payments?

GEEK Speak:

"A man builds a fine house; and now he has a master, and a task for life: he is to furnish, watch, show it, and keep it in repair, the rest of his days."
Ralph Waldo Emerson

- Responsibility – Paying for a home is not the only big responsibility that comes with ownership. You have to be willing to keep your property in good repair, and make sure it looks nice for your sake and for those that live nearby. In addition, you must be ready to be a responsible neighbor. Are you willing to do your part in living harmoniously alongside others?

Give all of these items the thought they deserve. Better to think about them now than to wish you had later, when it's too late to turn back.

Because buying a home is such an important decision, let's be sure and look at both sides. There are some risks, too. Here are a few to consider:

- Expense – Your monthly payment may be more than what you have been paying for rent. Be sure you can afford the higher payments before you commit to them.

- Responsibility – As the owner, you will have to handle any problem that occurs. If you need a new roof, you'll have to pay for it. If you need new plumbing, you'll have to take care of hiring someone to replace it. If an appliance wears out, you'll have to bear the expense of getting a new one.

- Mobility – Once you accept the responsibility of home ownership, you will probably have to sell your home before you can move anywhere else. That may present a problem if you're transferred with your job, or have to relocate quickly. If your home hasn't sold by the time you move, you'll be forced to try to maintain the home and sell it from a distance, which is not always easy. Think about the flexibility you'll give up—if you think you might need to move soon, put off buying a home.

- Depreciation – You may buy a home thinking you'll make money on it when you sell it, but that's not always the case. Sometimes you can lose money because of things you should have done and didn't, like not keeping up with repairs and maintenance. But sometimes, even if you do everything right, the home can lose its value because of factors outside of your control, such as a recession, or decreasing property values in the neighborhood as a whole.

Carefully consider the pros and the cons before deciding to purchase a home.

As you can see, there are numerous issues to evaluate before you rush into buying a home. Take time to think through each one carefully before you proceed.

 **GEEK AT A GLANCE**

- There are compelling financial reasons to buy a home. In particular, it puts your money to work for you and may offer some tax advantages. Plus, your money is buying something you can own, instead of just paying rent.

- There are more subjective reasons to consider as well, such as need, affordability, and timing.

- There are also some negatives to home buying, such as mortgage payments that are usually higher than rent, and the burden of being responsible for repairs when they are needed.

- You should carefully consider every facet of home buying before you begin the process.

PREPARING FOR THE PURCHASE

Once you've made the decision to pursue home ownership, the best thing you can do to make this a smooth process is to get your finances in order.

You might think it's putting the cart before the horse to talk about how to pay for a house before you even find one you want to buy, but you can't buy a home unless your finances are in good shape. If they're not, it won't matter how many houses you find to buy.

Here's how to get ready to buy your dream home:

- Request a copy of your credit report to make sure there are no problems or errors in your credit history that will prevent you from getting a mortgage. More about how to do that in the next chapter.

- Gather records that you will need. Here are some documents you'll have to present to get a mortgage:

  - W-2s and tax returns for last two years
  - If self-employed, tax returns for 2 years, plus a year-to-date profit and loss statement (P & L—also simply called an income statement)
  - Checking account statements for last 2 months
  - Statements from any other accounts for last 2 months, including savings, IRAs, and money markets
  - Pay stubs for last 2 months

GUERRILLA GEEK

If you are self-employed or have an irregular income, you will usually need to provide information about your various accounts for the past three years. You may need to check with a lender who specializes in dealing with people in your situation.

- Evidence of other assets, such as CDs, bonds, and stocks
- Records of any derogatory credit history that has since been paid off
- Social Security numbers for all parties buying the house

Here are some other factors you'll need to be prepared to document as you proceed:

- Employment history – Lenders typically consider two years of steady work in the same industry as employment stability.

- Current debt – You'll need to document balances on loans for cars, jewelry, credit cards, or other items.

GEEKOID

As you gather information about your various accounts and other assets, keep in mind any activity happening in those accounts. Don't transfer any large amounts of money in or out while you're home shopping.

GEEK☉ID

Be sure not to go into even more debt while you're looking for your dream home. Mortgages are based on debt-to-income ratios, and more than one hopeful mortgage applicant has been stopped in his or her tracks by the new car they just purchased. Also, to improve your overall credit picture, pay off minor debts before you try to get a mortgage.

- Rent history – Name, address, and contact information for your landlord, amount of rent, and previous landlords over a two-year period.

- Current home information – If you already own a home, have ready the address, current market value, mortgage lender name, account number, current payment, and outstanding balance.

 *Gather the documents you will need to apply for a mortgage early in the house-hunting process. This can help speed up your loan approval later.*

In very particular circumstances, you will also need these items:

- If you are separated or divorced, you'll need legal documentation in the form of a divorce decree or separation agreement. You must also bring documentation of child support payments if you want these to be included in your income.

GUERRILLA GEEK

If you've decided to buy a home, it may be helpful for you to look around and locate a homebuyer education class. Many real estate agencies and community groups offer them.

- If you are receiving public assistance as part of your income (such as disability insurance, or Social Security), you will need to document the amount.

- If you have ever declared bankruptcy, gone through foreclosure, or had any other credit-related judgments against you over the past seven years, you will have to produce documentation of the proceedings.

GEEKOID

As you evaluate what you want in a house, be sure to also take into consideration what you will need in the foreseeable future. Don't under-buy. For instance, if you plan on starting a family soon, make sure you buy enough house to accommodate the new arrival.

So now that you're in the market for a home, here are a few other words to the wise:

- Be an informed buyer. Research your particular area to learn about the schools, location to work, and other variables that affect property value—to you and others. Some things you'll want to keep abreast of are the following:
- current interest rates
- current house prices in your target area, including asking and sales prices
- circumstances that may affect certain locations, such as new zoning regulations or road projects that may mean unwanted traffic

- Be realistic. Start now to distinguish between what you want in a house and what you actually need. Don't stretch your budget thin paying for features you really won't use that much.

- Do not hesitate to ask questions about anything in the process. There are no stupid questions. You are getting ready to make one of the biggest decisions of your life, and you deserve to have all the information you need.

- Prepare for the long haul. You may find the right house on the first day you look, or on the hundredth. Either way, be patient and remember that the goal is to get the best home for you and your family, not just to get one quickly. Don't settle for something that you may regret later. You'll enjoy the destination later, but for now, try to enjoy the journey.

GEEK
AT A GLANCE

- Getting your finances in order is the first step to home buying.

- Request a copy of your credit report to make sure there will be no problems to prevent you from getting a mortgage.

- Correct any errors you find in the report, and clear up any problems that exist.

- Gather important documents you will need when you apply for a mortgage, such as recent tax returns and pay stubs, plus statements of assets.

- Confirm your employment history and your current debt in writing.

- Be ready to explain specific financial situations that may pose a problem, such as a bankruptcy or foreclosure in your past.

- Be an informed buyer. Learn all you can about the process before you begin.

- Prepare for the long haul. You may find something immediately, but be patient and wait for the right thing if it takes a while.

GETTING TO THE CORE OF YOUR CREDIT SCORE

One of the first things you'll need to do to get ready to buy a house is to check your credit score. This is because you will probably need to get a mortgage to pay for your new home.

Your credit score is the single most important factor in deciding the interest rate you will pay for getting a mortgage.

The information in a credit report is collected by credit bureaus, who then offer it to potential creditors. There are three main reporting agencies: Equifax, TransUnion, and Experian. Their reports don't say if you're a good risk, but they do offer information to help a creditor make a decision about that.

 *Your credit score is the single most important factor in what interest rate you'll pay for a mortgage.*

One way this is done is by assigning you a credit score, a three-digit number that takes into account all the information in your credit history. The numbers range from 300 to 850, with the higher number indicating a better credit risk.

Here's how the score is determined: Points are assigned based on items in your credit history. The resulting score is compared to that of other consumers with similar profiles. With this information, lenders can predict how likely someone is to repay a loan and make payments on time.

GEEKOID

A potential lender isn't the only person who might ask permission to obtain a copy of your credit report. Prospective employers also often do so as a means to verify information provided by applicants, and to learn information that the applicant might not offer. Most employers request a credit check to check a job candidate's responsibility, as indicated by how he or she pays bills, to verify employment history, and to determine the likelihood for workplace theft.

Although there are several scoring methods, the one most commonly used by lenders is known as a FICO® score, named for Fair Isaac and Company, an independent company that created it. Another popular company is Beacon. Here's what usually goes into the score:

Payment history – 35 percent
Amounts owed – 30 percent
Length of credit history – 15 percent
New credit – 10 percent
Types of credit used – 10 percent

Other factors include the number and type of inquiries, and public records, including bankruptcy filings. If you have a large number of new credit inquiries, this will affect your score because it looks like you're preparing to go into more debt by getting new loans.

However, inquiries for the purpose of getting a mortgage do not affect your credit score this way. All mortgage inquiries within a

GEEKOID

Be careful not to base your expectations for a mortgage on a credit score that you get from the Internet. Typically, FICO® scores are anywhere from 35 to 100 points below a generic score purchased from an Internet site.

thirty-day period count as one inquiry. This was designed so that you can shop for mortgage rates and not be penalized.

Even if you are able to get a mortgage despite a poor credit score, you'll pay more for it than someone with a better score. Here's an example, taken from FICO®'s website that illustrates how a poor credit score can hurt you. Using a $150,000 30-year, fixed-rate mortgage, here's a comparison of how much you'll pay for your mortgage if you have a good credit rating, as opposed to a poor one.

Your FICO® Score	Your interest rate	Your monthly payment
760 – 850	5.46%	$848
700 – 759	5.68%	$869
680 – 699	5.86%	$885
660 – 679	6.07%	$906
640 – 659	6.5%	$948
620 – 639	7.05%	$1,003

You can see from the chart that having bad credit could cost you as much as $150 more a month for a mortgage, if you can get one.

GUERRILLA GEEK

You are always allowed a free copy of a credit report directly from one of the three agencies if you've recently been turned down for credit, insurance, or employment based on your credit score. The company turning you down must notify you of which agency provided the information. You are also eligible for a free copy if you've been the victim of identity theft. With all of these circumstances, you have sixty days from the time of the adverse report in which to request your free copy.

Getting a Copy of Your Credit Report

You can easily check your own credit report to see what's in it before anyone else does, so you can begin to correct any problems that might be there. Thanks to a recent amendment to the federal Fair Credit Reporting Act, you can request a free copy of your credit report from each of the three reporting agencies once every twelve months. Simply contact the Annual Credit Report Request Service at www.annualcreditreport.com. You may also contact them by phone or mail:

Toll-free number: 877-322-8228
Mail: Annual Credit Report Request Service
            P.O. Box 105281
            Atlanta, GA 30348-5281

If you need to check with each agency more than once a year, you can get a copy at any time by requesting one at the website of any or all of the three agencies, by calling their toll-free numbers, or by mailing in a form obtained at www.ftc.gov/credit. Here is contact information for each of the three agencies:

Equifax
www.equifax.com
800-685-1111

TransUnion
www.transunion.com
800-916-8800

Experian
www.experian.com
888-397-3742 (888-EXPERIAN)

GEEKOID

Inquiries that you authorized, such as those from mortgage companies, are visible to anyone requesting a copy of your credit report. Inquiries by unauthorized companies like credit card companies, who get only a partial credit report for the purpose of pre-qualifying you for a credit card, can be seen only by you. These do not count against your credit score.

GUERRILLA GEEK

Each late payment you've made to a creditor lowers your credit score more than the previous one. So even if you're thirty days late on a payment, go ahead and make the payment as soon as possible before it goes to sixty days. After ninety days a late payment becomes a judgment, and will also be included. If you've had a bankruptcy, it will appear on your report, and may make it almost impossible to get a loan.

What You'll Find on Your Credit Report

Each of the three credit bureaus may have slightly different information on their reports, but most major accounts, like a car loan, should appear on all three. Here are some pieces of information you should find on all reports:

- Identifying information: This will include your name, nickname, personal information such as date of birth and Social Security number, current and previous employers, and contact information such as your phone number, plus current and past addresses.

- Credit information: The report will provide specific information about each account you have, such as the date opened, credit limit or loan amount, balance, monthly payment, and payment pattern during the last several years. Information about your payment history remains in your credit report for up to seven years. Information from public records such as bankruptcies can remain in your report for up to ten years.

- Public record information: Not only will obvious information such as bankruptcies be included, but so will tax liens, monetary judgments, and in some states, overdue child support.

- Inquiries: This will include the names of all those who have obtained a copy of your credit report for any reason. Inquiries remain on the report for up to two years, as outlined by federal law.

Improving Your Credit Score

If your credit report indicates that you are not in as good a shape as you should be to qualify, there are things you can do.

- One obvious thing to do is to check for inaccuracies on your report that may be bringing down your score, and correct them. It may take thirty days or longer for the correction to show up, but monitor the situation closely to be sure your credit history reflects the change.

- Identify the accounts on which you legitimately owe money, call the companies, and offer to pay the balance if they'll take the negative information off your report. On accounts that you've already paid off, but have had a spotty repayment history, call and ask the company to remove the information from your report since the account is paid in full.

- Pay off as many credit card balances as you can, but don't close those accounts. How much you owe relative to your total credit limit is a significant factor in your credit score, and you should keep your balances at or below about 25 percent of your card limits.

- Get current on all your bills and stay that way. Pay everything on time.

- Ask one of your credit card companies to raise your credit limit. This will lower your percentage of credit used in relation to your credit available, which helps your score. Just be sure you don't increase your balance after your limit is raised, because that could actually hurt you instead of helping you.

Once you've cleaned up your report as much as you can, here are some ways to help you get a fresh start on your credit.

- Get a secured credit card. This is a card that has a credit limit, and for which an amount equal to your limit is held in the bank. Since the bank has the money in hand each month as you use your card, and then pay it off, it isn't taking any risk. After about a year, if you have made payments completely and on time, the bank will return the money it was holding to secure the card.

GEEKOID

Only your repayment history is reflected on your credit report. Bounced checks won't be included, but they will put your name in a national system accessed by merchants who may stop accepting your checks.

- Ask a friend or family member to cosign a loan with you. Then be sure to pay it back on time to help repair your credit history. After about a year of paying, you can ask the financial institution to remove the other person's name, leaving only yours.

- Get a card that is easy to get, such as a department store credit card.

GUERRILLA GEEK

Since credit bureaus have such an impact on your ability to get a mortgage, you may be interested to know a little about how they got started. Surprisingly, they had very humble beginnings. When people first started to buy things on credit, store clerks would write the purchase on a piece of paper, then put the paper in a "cuff," a paper tube worn on the clerk's wrist. Eventually someone had the idea of collecting the information for other potential lenders to see. Even though no effort was made to verify the information for accuracy, it covered a wide range of information, and included even character references and driving records. The information was originally offered to local businesses. It wasn't until the 1830s that third party reporting agencies were formed to offer the information on a broader scale. The information has continued to become increasingly available as communication equipment has been developed to disperse it.

GEEK
AT A GLANCE

- The first thing to do when getting your finances in order is to check your credit report.

- Information contained in the report is collected by credit bureaus and then offered to potential creditors.

- The report does not say whether you are a good credit risk; it offers information to allow creditors to make their own judgment.

- One thing the report provides is a three-digit number that takes into account all information in your report. This is your credit score. It will be between 300 and 850, with higher numbers indicating better risks.

- The most commonly used scoring method is known as a FICO® because it was developed by Fair Isaac and Company.

- You are entitled to one free copy of your credit report per year from each of the three major reporting agencies: Equifax, TransUnion, and Experian.

- Immediately correct erroneous information in your credit report.

- If your credit score is lower than you expected, take steps to improve it. Get and stay current on your bills, and ask at least one company to raise your credit limit.

ESTIMATING YOUR EXPENSES EASILY

The biggest question you'll face right up front is, "How much can I afford?"

The next question you'll want an answer for is, "How much cash will I need?" The answers are relatively simple to calculate. This chapter will give you a brief overview to get you going in the right direction. You can find more in-depth explanations in later chapters.

Decide How Much You Can Afford

Calculating how much house you can afford may seem like a daunting task; however, it's actually very simple using a couple of methods. One is based on your current yearly income, and the other is based on how much you think you can afford monthly.

First, let's get an estimate based on your income. A general rule of thumb when deciding what price house to purchase is to multiply your gross yearly income by 3. This will give you a general starting point for the home price that you can afford.

GEEK*Speak:*

"No money is better spent than what is laid out for domestic satisfaction."

Samuel Johnson

Here is an example of how this works:

$50,000 yearly income
x 3
$150,000 home price

Using this formula, if you have an annual income of $50,000, you could afford a house priced at about $150,000. Remember that this is a general rule to use to see what price home you should look at based on a guideline to pay no more than 35 percent of your income on housing.

Now, to see how that breaks down to monthly payments, take an honest look at your finances to determine what you think you can afford. A mortgage company is looking at the hard numbers when determining what you will qualify for but only you can decide what you are willing to spend for housing. You are the only one who would know that you can't live without your $6 latte every morning. Many times a lender will tell you that you will qualify for much more than you can really comfortably afford to pay.

There's an easy way to test how much more you can afford each month for housing before you actually commit to it. Simply take the estimate of the larger payment that you think you can make; pay your regular rent/house payment; then put the difference in a savings account so that you actually are making the larger payment. For example:

$1200 approximate mortgage payment
$700 current rent
$500 difference to savings per month

Try this out for several months to see how it fits in your budget. If you're comfortable making the larger payment, then you'll be more confident about your ability to pay a larger house payment on a permanent basis. Plus, you'll have extra money in your savings account thanks to your little experiment.

Once you've decided how much monthly payment you think you can swing, you can easily estimate what house price that translates to. Find out what the going interest rate is for mortgages (check

PMI stands for Private Mortgage Insurance, which is extra insurance often required by lenders for homeowners who make a down payment of less than 20 percent.

online or in the newspaper for up-to-date information). Then use a mortgage payment table or an Excel spreadsheet to calculate what a payment would be.

A good rule of thumb is that for every $1,000 in price, your payment will be $70. This is very inexact, but gives you an estimate. For example, a $100,000 house will be roughly $700 a month. That's before taxes, insurance, and any PMI; to cover those, add another $100-$300.

So if you think you can afford $1,000 a month, you're probably looking at a $130,000 house. After a 20 percent down payment, you'd be financing roughly $104,000. Once you begin to shop around for a mortgage, the potential lenders can give you more precise information.

Decide How Much Cash You'll Need

The total cost of the house, and even the monthly payment you can expect, are not the only amounts you'll need to know. You will also need to know how much cash you'll need up front. Different loan products require different amounts for down payment. These are discussed in more detail in the chapter on different types of mortgages, but this will give you a good ballpark figure for how much cash you'll need to start this process.

GUERRILLA GEEK

The less cash you're putting into the deal, the pickier the mortgage company will be about how much money you have in savings, your credit score, and other details. They just want to make sure you have something invested, making it less likely you'll walk away and leave them with a house to sell.

The details are provided below, but you can estimate that you'll need your down payment—anywhere from 3 to 20 percent—plus about 3 percent for closing costs and prepaids. For example, to buy a $100,000 house, you'd need $20,000 down (if paying 20 percent down), plus another $3,000 for closing costs and prepaids. So you'd need about $23,000. If you're short on cash and want to pay only 3 percent down, you'll need about $6,000. And since you can sometimes ask the seller to pay your closing costs and prepaids, you can get in a house with as little as $3,000.

While your down payment amount depends on what type of loan you are obtaining, there are fees that are generally incurred for any loan: closing costs and prepaids.

Don't be put off by all these items. Just remember that the loan origination fee is usually 1 percent, and all the other stuff usually adds up to about 2 percent, giving you 3 percent total. Here are some typical expenses you'll face at closing:

GEEKOID

One way to reduce the amount of money you will need at closing is to increase the price you are willing to pay for a house and have the seller pay your closing costs. For example, if you are willing to pay $100,000 for a house, offer the seller $103,500 and ask the seller to pay $3,500 of your closing costs and prepaids. This will allow you to keep your savings intact so that you will have extra funds after closing to make changes to the house as well as update items as you like.

You will also need less cash at closing if you close on the last day of the month. That is because the mortgage company collects interest from the date you close until the last day of the month. If you close on the 15th, you have to pay 15 days of interest at closing. Just be sure you're aware of this if you're short on cash.

Costs of Obtaining a Loan:
> Loan origination fee
> Loan discount fee (points)
> Appraisal fee*
> Credit report fee*
> Lender's inspection fee
> Mortgage broker fee
> Tax related service fee
> Processing fee
> Underwriting fee
> Wire transfer fee
> Application fee

GEEK☉ID

An HUD-1 Settlement Statement is a form used by the settlement agent to itemize all charges imposed upon a borrower and seller for a real estate transaction. It gives both parties a full understanding of their incoming and outgoing funds. You will get a copy of this at closing.

Title Insurance and Attorney's Fees:
    Attorney fee (also called escrow or closing fee)
    Document prep fee
    Notary fees
    Title insurance (purchaser's policy)

Government Recording and Transfer Fees:
    Recording fees
    City and/or county tax/stamps
    State tax/stamps

Other Fees:
    Flood Certification fee*
    Survey
    Termite inspection and bond transfer

Fees listed above with an asterisk may be charged at application and will be credited as paid on the HUD-1 at closing. These fees are often referred to as POC: paid outside of closing.

You will also be asked to pay some expenses that are called prepaids because they are paid at closing for a future bill. Here are some items in that category:

GEEK⊙ID

If you're currently renting, you'll get a month with no payment when you buy a house. That's because rents are paid up front, meaning you pay for January's rent on January 1. If you close on a house on January 31, your first payment won't be due until March 1. Mortgages are paid in arrears. That means your first month is free—a great relief to most first-time buyers.

- one year of hazard insurance
- taxes that are paid into your escrow account at closing for the next year's tax bill
- interest you pay from the day you close through the end of that month (none, if you close on the last day of the month).

Another important part of determining your price range will be handled by getting pre-qualified or pre-approved. More about that later.

GEEK*Speak:*

"Owning a home is a keystone of wealth ... both financial affluence and emotional security."

Suze Orman

GEEK AT A GLANCE

- There are two main questions you'll want answered concerning money for buying a house: "How much can I afford?" and "How much cash will I need?"

- Estimate how much house you can afford by multiplying your income by 3 to get the price-range you can afford.

- You can also determine how much house you can afford by identifying the amount of payment you could pay monthly— for every $70 you can pay, you can afford $1,000 in price.

- When figuring monthly payments, allow another $100-300 for taxes, insurance, and other extra costs.

- You should pay only about 35 percent of your monthly income for housing.

- These formulas are only designed to give rough estimates. You should check with a lender or a real estate agent for more precise numbers.

LOOKING FOR A MONEY TREE

If you're like most people, you will need to borrow money to help you buy a home. That means you'll get a mortgage, or a loan, to make your purchase.

You may think you should wait until you actually find the home you want to shop around for a lender, but it's best to do this early in the process.

There are a couple of reasons for this. The first is that the lender can pre-qualify or pre-approve you as a buyer before you even begin to look for houses, which will put you in a much stronger position to negotiate. Second, you can go ahead and lay the groundwork for the mortgage process so that when you do find a house, you'll only need to add the particulars to the information you've already provided to the lender, which will facilitate closing.

GEEK GLOSSARY

A **mortgage** is a long-term loan that you obtain to cover the purchase price of a home. You may get the loan from a bank, mortgage company, credit union, or other source.

Let's take a look at the types of places that offer mortgages, and see what each has to offer.

Mortgage Companies

Mortgage companies usually have the broadest spectrum of mortgage products. They generally have many investors to which

In the word **mortgage**, *mort-* is from the Latin word for death, and *–gage* means a pledge to forfeit something of value if a debt is not repaid. So mortgage is a "dead pledge" for two reasons: the property was "dead" to the borrower if the loan was not repaid, and the pledge was "dead" if the loan was repaid.

they sell loans, giving them the luxury of offering many different mortgage products. Mortgage companies are solely in the business of providing home loans and as such, are specialists in this area. They will also work after hours and on weekends. Loan originators are paid on commission and therefore it is in their best interest for you to obtain a loan.

Banks

Your local bank can also be a good source of funds. You probably already have a relationship with a bank if you have a checking or savings account. Banks will typically have a few specialized programs tailored to certain groups. For example, they usually have a special program for medical and law students, whereby they will give them a loan based on their future earning potential as opposed to their current income. While this situation certainly doesn't apply to everyone, they may have other programs available that fit your needs.

Banks are typically conservative with their credit terms, meaning they may have stricter guidelines for debt-to-income ratios and required credit scores. Bank originators are typically salaried, meaning they get paid the same amount no matter how many loans

GEEKID

The first savings bank in the United States was the Philadelphia Savings Fund Society, established on December 20, 1816.

they originate or close in a given month. They are typically only available during regular business hours, but they may make themselves available on weekends for special circumstances.

Savings and Loan Associations

Commonly called S&Ls, these offer primarily residential mortgages. Many make home lending their main business, and they offer low rates. They were popular awhile back, but underwent changes in the late '70s and '80s.

GEEKOID

Savings and loan institutions have existed since the 1800s. They were originally community-based institutions for savings and mortgages.

Credit Unions

As with a bank you may also have a relationship with a credit union. Some credit unions offer home loans, but not all of them do. They typically offer only one or two different specialized programs, but if those meet your needs, they typically have better rates and lower fees than banks and mortgage companies. They sometimes have lower minimum down payment requirements with no PMI.

Mortgage Brokers

Mortgage brokers act like a clearing house for mortgage seekers. They do not make loans themselves. Rather, they keep tabs on the mortgage market through ties to local and national lenders, and are then able to refer mortgage applicants to lenders with terms suitable to them.

GEEK GLOSSARY

Good Faith Estimate: A summary of all the costs involved in getting a mortgage.

Mortgage brokers can be especially helpful if you have unusual mortgage needs. They can take your application and compile all documents necessary for processing. Then they can counsel you on the best products to meet your needs, and finally pass your file on to the lender who can best serve you. Because they have access to many different lenders, mortgage brokers are more likely to find a loan to meet your particular needs. Also, because of the nature of their business, brokers are experts at shopping the market and can advise you on your best option.

Brokers are usually paid by customers by adding in a markup on prices quoted from the lender. This may be in the form of a markup of one or more points to be added to the closing fees.

Comparison of Your Options

The bottom line is that you need to check with all available sources before finding a home mortgage to be sure you get the best deal for your situation. One of the best tools to use when deciding between mortgage products is a good faith estimate, often referred to as a GFE. This cost estimate is the only way to really compare the actual cost to obtain a mortgage. This will list the annual percentage rate the lender is charging for a loan, all of the fees they are charging, as well as estimates of all of the services required to obtain a mortgage.

After you've obtained a GFE from a lender, they cannot legally charge you more for interest or any of the fees listed on this report. Note that the cost of services, such as surveys, credit reports, or appraisals, may change, since those costs are out of the lender's control. You can request a GFE before going to the application process to help you decide which lender to choose.

GEEK AT A GLANCE

- You should begin early to shop for a mortgage lender.

- Look at various institutions and compare what they have to offer. Options would include mortgage companies, banks, savings and loans, credit unions, and mortgage brokers.

- Each different type of lender has its own benefits and limitations.

- The best comparison is to get a GFE (good faith estimate) from each lender you consider. Then you compare the various GFEs to see where you can find the mortgage right for you.

GETTING APPROVAL FROM OTHERS

The first reason it's best to go ahead and start the mortgage process is so you can get pre-qualified or pre-approved, and be in a much better position to look at houses.

Either of these processes can help you confirm whether you have correctly estimated how much house you can afford, and will also offer assurance to the seller that you can afford to buy his house. This can give you a huge advantage as a buyer. In addition, if you've overestimated how much house you can afford, it can spare you the disappointment of getting your heart set on a particular home, and then finding out later that you can't afford it.

It's simple. Just go to one of the lending institutions mentioned in the previous chapter and ask to be pre-qualified or pre-approved. Let's take a look at what each of these designations has to offer.

Pre-qualification

Getting pre-qualified means that you have told a lender your income level and your debt and credit information, and the lender has estimated what you can afford. You will receive a pre-qualification letter, which is a statement from a mortgage lender that you are approved for a loan amount based on the facts that you have given regarding your credit and income. At this point the lender has taken an application but has not verified your income or credit.

GEEKOID

You are not required to get your mortgage from the same institution that pre-qualified or pre-approved you. If you want to get pre-qualified/pre-approved and then take more time to shop for a mortgage, you may do so.

While this is certainly a start, it is viewed only as tentative approval since no in-depth analysis of your financial condition is done. While the institution selected takes the information, it does not verify it. And the pre-qualification letter can be withdrawn later if the company discovers significant negative factors.

GUERRILLA GEEK

Getting pre-qualified does nothing to lock in an interest rate, which is an important factor that will affect the final amount of your monthly mortgage payments.

Pre-approval

Pre-approval puts you in a much stronger stance for buying. It means that the lender has taken your financial information, has verified your employment and income, has checked your credit report as well as your debt-to-income ratio, and has actually analyzed your financial situation.

The only thing the company cannot verify at this point is, of course, the actual house you intend to buy, since you have not found it yet. The company will issue a pre-approval letter to express its guarantee of a loan approval for a specific amount. This letter is a firm commitment from the mortgage company that they have reviewed your credit and income and will guarantee that you are approved for a mortgage up to a predetermined amount as long as the property you choose is acceptable and no other variables change.

This letter will certainly take more time to get than the pre-qualification statement because the lender will evaluate your application, secure a credit check, and verify other information such as your employment and account information. Then the application is sent to underwriting where secondary lenders check it and give their approval. The process might take only a few days, but it will take a little longer if any problems are discovered along the way.

Allowing time to resolve any problems that may be found in the mortgage process is another good reason to start early in your house hunting. Whether the problems are genuine, or whether they incorrectly appear in your records, they can take time to correct. This is also a good reason to check your own credit record—to take care of any problems in advance and prepare the way for a smooth home buying process.

GEEKOID

Some companies do not charge any fee for pre-approval, though some ask that the applicant cover the fee for a credit report. Be sure to ask up front what fees are involved.

GEEKOID

If you're short on time, you might be offered a preliminary pre-approval letter. This means that your application has been taken, and your credit has been checked, but the underwriting has not been done yet.

Other problems that might arise could be lack of enough income to qualify for the amount you wanted, or maybe a bigger down payment will be required than you anticipated and planned for. It's best to know these things ahead of time. Getting pre-approved

Pre-approval letters are usually valid for a period of sixty to ninety days.

can assure the seller that you are a legitimate buyer and there are no problems for him to worry about.

Attaching a pre-approval letter to an offer to purchase property may make your offer more attractive than an offer without a pre-approval. Keep this in mind since your offer may be presented to a seller with other offers in an aggressive housing market. Your offer will be a sure thing, whereas the unapproved buyers' will not be.

Both processes make you a more appealing buyer to a seller. However, pre-approval is certainly the more secure of the two.

GEEKOID

A lot of people get pre-approved for a mortgage and then buy a new car or change jobs. This can often ruin your chances of getting a mortgage, since your pre-approval is based on your situation at that point in time. So be sure to check with your mortgage company before making any financial decisions while waiting to buy a home.

GEEK AT A GLANCE

- Contact a mortgage company early in the home buying process.

- One of the first things a mortgage company can do for you is to pre-qualify or pre-approve you as a buyer.

- Being pre-qualified means that you have reported your income and credit information to a mortgage company and it has estimated how much house you can afford.

- Being pre-approved means you have given detailed financial information to a lending agency, which has run a credit report and done a financial analysis to determine how much home you can buy.

- Both processes make you an attractive buyer, but being pre-approved is the better of the two options, and makes you a much more attractive buyer.

APPLYING YOURSELF

You will be well ahead of the game if you apply for a mortgage as soon as you select a lender.

You do not have to have a property chosen to start the application process. You will simply give permission for your credit report to be pulled by the lender, and begin the process that will be completed when you have decided on a home to purchase.

This is where all that paperwork you gathered comes in. The lender will want to know a lot of information about you, and will ask for details about all your sources of income, debts, and above all, your credit history. If you have taken steps earlier to gather everything, and especially to check to see that your credit report is in good shape, the mortgage process will get off to a smooth start.

GUERRILLA GEEK

The Consumer Credit Protection Act was passed by Congress in 1968 to require creditors to reveal the cost of getting a loan. Also called the Truth in Lending Act, it requires lenders to disclose terms and costs of all loans, including the annual percentage rate, points, and fees; the total principle being financed; payment due and terms; the application fee; any annual or one-time service fees; prepayment penalties; the property's address; key features of variable-rate loans; total finance charges; and whether the loan is assumable.

Once you meet the lender's requirements, you will become pre-approved for a mortgage up to a certain amount. We've already discussed how beneficial it will be to your home search if you are pre-qualified and especially pre-approved.

There will be many documents that you will be required to sign during the mortgage process. This section should give you more confidence when signing these documents.

GEEKOID

When you apply for a mortgage, you may be asked to pay an application fee, credit report fee, and an appraisal fee.

- The first form is the application. This will be the basis of your loan. It includes your name, employer, manner in which you want to hold title, property address, as well as lists all of your assets and liabilities. You will also be provided with an initial Truth in Lending, usually called a TIL. The TIL will give you an APR as well as show you an estimated payment based on the loan product and loan amount that you are applying for.

If you followed instructions in the previous chapters about checking your credit, clearing up problems in your credit report, and gathering important papers you will need, you will have no problems when applying for a mortgage.

- If you've already found the property you want to buy when you apply for the mortgage, you'll be asked to sign upfront disclosures or 72 hour docs. These are required to be provided by the mortgage company within 72 hours of application.

Be honest and thorough when preparing your loan application. Errors and incomplete information will only slow the process.

- The mortgage lender will also provide you with a Good Faith Estimate (GFE), often called a summary of costs, and a copy of the fee schedule for you to review. A GFE is the best way for you to compare apples to apples when comparing mortgage products and companies. Mortgage company fees cannot be charged on the HUD-1 at closing unless they are disclosed on the GFE.

- You will be given a servicing disclosure that will give you a percentage of loans that the mortgage company sells to another investor.

Among the items listed on your GFE (Good Faith Estimate), you may see a reference to **discount points** or simply **points**. Points are equal to 1 percent of the amount borrowed. They are considered as prepaid interest, payable in advance, that are fully tax deductible for first-time home buyers in the year of purchase. For repeat home buyers and home owners just wanting to refinance, the points are tax deductible over the life of the loan.

GUERRILLA GEEK

Here's a summary of what you should bring when applying for a mortgage.

- Required: Pay stubs, bank statements, contract and cancelled earnest money check if you have already found your house

- Supporting: W-2 forms, income tax returns, corporate tax returns and profit/loss statements, income verification if self-employed, gift fund documents, divorce documents, bankruptcy papers, military eligibility certificates, current landlord information

- You will also sign a disclosure that gives the mortgage company permission to pull your credit. The mortgage company will disclose to you any company with which they have a business relationship; this is usually called the affiliated business relationship disclosure.

- You may be required to sign a lock-in agreement. This document tells you the interest rate at which they have locked you in, and will express any lock-in fee that you have incurred for an extended lock-in rate. This is extremely important, because this rate cannot be changed without incurring fees. If rates go up or down between the time you sign this and buy a house, you are still locked in to this rate. This is good if rates go up, but you might not be happy with it if rates go down.

GEEK GLOSSARY

A **lock-in rate** is a lender's promise to honor a certain rate and certain number of points for a specified amount of time while your loan is being processed. This protects you if the rate goes up between the time you apply for the loan and the time you close. However, it will also prevent you from taking advantage of any decrease in rate that might occur during that time. Be sure to get this agreement in writing.

Some companies offer you a one-time float down—this is a feature that you should look for if a slight fluctuation bothers you. This allows you to lock in the interest rate and points at some time after application but before settlement. Generally, rates don't dramatically rise or fall in a short period of time, so this isn't something that should keep you up at night. Just know your own comfort level with this before signing it.

Other documents that a mortgage company may ask you to sign include a notice that you are to apply for homeowner's insurance and

GEEKOID

Lock-ins of thirty to sixty days are common, but some may be for as few as seven days, while others may be for four months. Lenders that charge a lock-in fee usually charge more for longer periods of time.

have that in place prior to closing. If you are applying for joint credit you will have to sign a document acknowledging that as well.

Once all your information is submitted, here are some items that will factor into the company's decision about whether you will be approved for a loan.

- Financial position – You must be in a sound financial situation to be a good credit risk.

- Gross income – As a very practical consideration, you must have enough money coming in to allow you to make mortgage payments and honor your other obligations at the same time. This will include not only your actual salary, but any commissions and bonuses you may receive, and other income such as that from rental properties, dividends, pensions, and social security.

- Sale of existing properties – This will include money from the sale of your current home that can be applied to your new home.

- Amount you can afford – Based on common industry formulas, the potential lender will determine the limits of the loan for which you may be qualified.

- Total debt – Your Total Debt Service Ratio (TDSR) ratio will be considered, which is the ratio of your debt to your total income.

- Creditworthiness – Based on your past credit history, you will be evaluated as to how likely you are to repay the loan in a responsible manner. Your credit history will be examined for pattern of repayment and to see whether there is a history of late payments.

- Property – If you have already selected the property you want to buy, the lender must be assured that it offers adequate value as security for the mortgage amount. A portion of this decision will be based on the appraiser's report detailing the estimated value of the residence as compared to nearby properties recently sold.

Following your application, you will receive one of four responses:

- Approval – The loan may be approved with no conditions or contingencies.

GUERRILLA GEEK

If a loan can be approved, but a condition must be met prior to closing, a "prior-to-funding" conditional approval will be given. In this case, the appropriate documents will be sent to the lawyer, but the lender will not fund the loan until the condition has been met. An example would be proof of the sale of an existing home when the equity in that home is needed for the purchase of the new home.

- Approved with conditions – If the underwriter needs additional documentation before a final decision can be made, you may be approved with conditions until the additional information is supplied.

- Suspended – In some cases, there is simply not enough information on which to base a decision about the loan. The file may be set aside until all the information can be provided by the applicant.

- Denial – If the applicant does not meet the minimum standards of the lender, the application may be denied. Some lenders require that a second underwriter review the loan package before a final denial is communicated to the buyer. Underwriting guidelines vary among lenders, so if you are denied a loan, check with another lender.

GEEK*Speak:*

"The ideal of happiness has always taken material form in the house, whether cottage or castle. It stands for permanence and separation from the world."

Simone de Beauvoir

 **GEEK AT A GLANCE**

- You may go ahead and begin the mortgage process even if you do not have a property selected yet. In fact, if your mortgage application is being processed as you look for a house, you will be ahead of the game once you have located the right property.

- There are numerous documents to complete when you apply for a mortgage. If you have already gathered all the information and records mentioned earlier, you will have everything you need to begin.

- You may be asked to pay some fees when you apply, including a fee for obtaining a copy of your credit report.

- You will receive several items in addition to copies of the documents you sign, including a Good Faith Estimate (GFE) and a service agreement from the lender.

THIS LOAN'S FOR YOU!

Deciding which mortgage is right for you can be a quick and easy decision.

Your mortgage company, bank, or credit union can offer advice on which is best for you, based on your current situation. But just so you know what they're talking about, here's an overview of the different products available.

Different Types of Mortgages

There are basically three different types of mortgages: FHA, VA, and conventional. Banks and mortgage companies offer all three. Credit unions usually handle only conventional loans.

FHA LOANS

FHA stands for Federal Housing Administration, which does not make home loans, but it has approved lenders who do, and then it insures the loans that are made. That means that if you fail to make your house payment, the FHA still gives the lenders their money.

FHA is part of the U.S. Department of Housing and Urban Development (HUD). One of its chief purposes is to help people obtain financing to buy their homes. It does this by allowing a

GEEKOID

FHA does not require that you have a credit score. Credit analysis may be completed using alternate credit sources such as your payment history for rent, car insurance, and utility bills.

GEEKOID

To make sure that FHA loans serve low- and moderate-income people, there are upper limits on the dollar value of the mortgage loan. Limits change every year, and vary by city and state. Check with your local lender to be sure you have updated information.

homebuyer to make a low down payment, and get a mortgage loan for the balance of the purchase price.

 It is important to note that FHA/HUD does not make loans directly to a homebuyer. You must go through a lending institution to get these loans.

Who qualifies? Almost anyone who has a good credit record, enough cash to pay closing costs, and sufficient and steady income to pay your monthly debts. For an FHA loan, your monthly housing costs (principal, interest, property taxes, and insurance) should generally not exceed 29 percent of your gross monthly income. Your total debt should not exceed 41 percent. There is no upper age limit for qualification, and no certain income level required, but individual mortgage amounts are limited by law. Generally, the home buyer applying for the loan must live in the home to get an FHA loan, that is, the loans are not available to investors.

Here is a chart that outlines the main points of FHA loans.

Maximum Purchase Price	FHA loans are limited based on purchase price. This amount varies from state to state, even county to county. Currently, the range is just above $200,000 to just over $350,000.
Minimum Down Payment	FHA loans can be worked many different ways, but usually the minimum investment is 3% of the sales price. This investment includes a minimum 2.25% down payment and .75% paid toward FHA allowable closing costs. Remember that this 3% investment may be borrowed. See below.
Debt-to-Income Ratios	Mortgage payment (PITI) should not exceed 29% of gross monthly income. Combined debts (PITI, car payments, credit cards) should not exceed 41% of gross monthly income. Car payments and other installment debts with more than 10 months remaining and all credit card debt is included.
Interest Rate	Interest rate will depend upon your credit score, but the rate is generally the same for FHA, VA, and conventional conforming loans.
Mortgage Insurance	Called MIP (mortgage insurance premium) for FHA loans. This rate changes based on your down payment.
Credit Score Requirements	There are no stated minimums, but most lenders agree that a borrower's credit score must be greater than 600 to get an FHA loan The higher your score, the lower the interest rate.
Seller Contributions	The seller can contribute up to 6% of the sales price toward the buyer's closing costs and prepaids.
Borrowed Funds	A buyer may borrow all funds needed for down payment, closing, and pre-paid costs as long as they are borrowed against an asset of the borrower, such as 401(k), stocks, bonds, or other real estate.
Gifts	Gifts for funds for down payment, closing costs, and prepaids may be obtained from a relative or someone with a clearly defined relationship. FHA allows all of the borrower's down payment, closing costs, and prepaids to be from a gift.
Wedding Registry	FHA allows buyers to set up an account at a bank or credit union to receive cash wedding gifts to be used toward the purchase of a house.
Is This the Loan for You?	If you have 3% to invest, have a fair credit score, are under the FHA maximum price cap, and the home needs few repairs or the seller is willing to make all the repairs before closing, then this is probably the loan for you.

GUERRILLA GEEK

FHA loans are available in urban and rural areas for the following types of homes:
- Single-family houses
- Houses with two, three, or four units
- Condominium units

VA LOANS

VA loans are available only to active and discharged veterans. Detailed information from the Department of Veterans Affairs' website is provided below to outline exactly who can get these loans.

To qualify for a VA loan, you must meet the requirements for eligibility.

Wartime

Service during WWII	Sept. 16, 1940 to July 25, 1947
Korean	June 27, 1950 to January 31, 1955
Vietnam	August 5, 1964 to May 7, 1975

GEEKOID

If you need help comparing loans, or advice on buying a home, you may call the HUD housing counseling and referral line toll-free at 1-800-569-4286 or may visit the HUD website at www.hud.gov. The web page also offers names of HUD-approved lenders.

GEEKOID

If you put less than 20 percent down on a house you will be required to pay mortgage insurance. This will be called PMI (Private Mortgage Insurance) for conventional loans, and MIP (Mortgage Insurance Premium) for FHA loans. This insurance is included in your monthly bill and you continue to pay it until the LTV (Loan to Value) drops below 80 percent. LTV is computed by dividing the principle loan amount by the value of a property. (For example, principle loan amount = $80,000 divided by property value = $100,000 has an 80 percent loan to value.) PMI can be avoided by having the lender pay this for you. This is called Lender Paid Mortgage Insurance. Your interest rate will be increased to cover this cost; however, interest is usually tax deductible whereas PMI is not. LPMI is paid over the life of the loan.

You must have served at least ninety days, and not have been dishonorably discharged. If you served less than ninety days, you may still be eligible if you were discharged for a service-related disability.

Peacetime
Service during   July 26, 1947 to June 26, 1950
February 1, 1955 to August 4, 1964
May 8, 1975 to September 7, 1980 (enlisted)
May 8, 1975 to October 16, 1981 (officer)

You must have served at least 181 days of continuous active duty and not have been dishonorably discharged. If you served less than 181 days, you may qualify if your discharge was due to a service related disability.

Service after September 7, 1980 (enlisted) or October 16, 1981 (officer)

If you were separated from service which began after these dates, you must have:

- Completed twenty-four months of continuous active duty or the full period (at least 181 days) for which you were ordered or called to active duty and been discharged under conditions other than dishonorable, or

- Completed at least 181 days of active duty and been discharged under the specific authority of 10 USC 1173 (Hardship), or 10 USC 1171 (Early Out), or have been determined to have a compensable service-connected disability, or

- Been discharged with less than 181 days of service for a service-connected disability. Individuals may also be eligible if they were released from active duty due to an involuntary reduction in force, certain medical conditions, or, in some instances, for the convenience of the government.

Gulf War – Service from August 2, 1990 to a date yet to be determined

If you served on active duty during the Gulf War, you must have:

- Completed twenty-four months of continuous active duty or the full period (at least ninety days) for which you were called or ordered to active duty, and been discharged under conditions other than dishonorable, or

- Completed at least ninety days of active duty and been discharged under the specific authority of 19 USC 1173 (Hardship), or 10 USC 1173 (Early Out), or have been determined to have a compensable service-connected disability, or

- Been discharged with less than ninety days of service for a service-connected disability. Individuals may also be eligible if they were released from active duty due to an involuntary reduction in force, certain medical conditions, or, in some instances, for the convenience of the government.

Active Duty Service Personnel

If you are not on regular duty (not active duty for training), you are eligible after having served eighteen days (ninety days during the Gulf War) unless discharged or separated from a previous qualifying period of active duty service.

GUERRILLA GEEK

If you have already been discharged from military service, the nature of your discharge will be critical to your qualification for a VA loan. If your discharge is classified as "other than honorable," seek help from your local VA office to learn what additional information you need to file, and what to do if an appeal is necessary.

Selected Reserves or National Guard

If you are not otherwise eligible, you may qualify if you have completed a total of six years in the Selected Reserves or National Guard (member of an active unit, attended required weekend drills, and two-week active duty for training) and

Congress passed the Serviceman's Readjustment Act, commonly known as the GI Bill of Rights, in 1944. One of its provisions enables the VA to help eligible people on active duty as well as veterans purchase homes.

- Were discharged with an honorable discharge, or
- Were placed on the retired list, or
- Were transferred to the Standby Reserve or an element of the Ready Reserve other than the Selected Reserve after service characterized as honorable service, or
- Continue to serve in the Selected Reserves.

Individuals who completed less than six years may be eligible if discharged for a service-connected disability.

You may also be eligible if you are an un-remarried spouse of a veteran who died while in service or from a service related disability, or are a spouse of a serviceperson missing in action or a prisoner of war.

Many people think they can get VA loans through the Department of Veterans Affairs, but that is not true. The Department does not issue those loans, but it does guarantee a portion of them against default. The guaranteed amount of a VA loan is called an entitlement. The current maximum entitlement for loans up to $144,000 is $36,000, with the exact figure being determined by your loan amount. The maximum entitlement for VA home loans that exceed $144,000 is $60,000.

Effective January 1, 2006, the VA home loan limit was increased to $417,000 for the forty-eight mainland states and Washington DC, and up to $625,000 in Alaska and Hawaii.

If you qualify, the best thing about a VA loan is that a buyer can actually purchase a home with a VA loan with absolutely no money out of pocket. You might only have to produce cash if you can't qualify for the monthly payments or if the cost of the property is more than the VA establishes as its "reasonable value."

You will, however, be responsible for closing costs: discount points, appraisal, credit report, survey, title search, and recording fees. You will also be responsible for a VA funding fee equal to 2.15 percent of the loan at settlement. This is reduced to 1.5 percent with a down payment of up to 10 percent, and 1.25 percent with a down payment of 10 percent or more. VA loans can be paid off at any time without penalty.

The following chart provides an overview of VA loans.

GEEKOID

If you have questions about qualifying for a VA loan, get a copy of your DD-214 and get in touch with the VA at www.va.gov, or by calling 1-800-827-1000.

Maximum Purchase Price	VA loans are limited by the maximum purchase price. This amount is currently $417,000 for no down payment, but is updated on an annual basis. The amount is higher if you have a down payment, but the only real benefit of a VA loan is the no-down-payment option. If you have a down payment, you're probably better off with a conventional loan.
Minimum Down Payment	No down payment is required for a VA loan.
Debt-to-Income Ratios	Combined debts (PITI, car payments, credit cards) should not exceed 41% of gross monthly income. Car payments and other installment debts with more than 10 months remaining and all credit card debt is included.
Interest Rate	Interest rate will depend upon your credit score, but the rate is generally the same for FHA, VA, and conventional conforming loans.
Mortgage Insurance	No mortgage insurance is required on a VA loan. However, in place of this there is an up-front VA funding fee. This fee is 2.14-2.4% for the first home purchased with a no down payment VA loan and 3.3% for any subsequent no down-payment home purchases using a VA loan. This funding fee can be added to the amount of the loan.
Credit Score Requirements	The VA does not have a stated minimum credit score, and they work with buyers who have had previous credit problems. While someone with a credit score below 600 is not a good candidate for a VA loan, they look mostly at your payment habits over the last 12-24 months, and do take into account special circumstances, like an extended illness.
Seller Contributions	The seller can contribute all of the buyer's closing costs and pre-paids, meaning no out-of-pocket cash is required of the buyer.
Borrowed Funds	A buyer may borrow all funds needed for down payment, closing, and pre-paid costs as long as they are borrowed against an asset of the borrower, such as 401(k), stocks, bonds, or other real estate. However, this is usually not necessary, because no cash is required for a VA loan.
Gifts	Gifts for funds for down payment, closing costs, and prepaids may be obtained from a relative or someone with a clearly defined relationship. This is usually not necessary because no cash is required for a VA loan.
Is This the Loan for You?	If you are an eligible veteran, have no money to invest, have a fair to good credit score, are under the VA maximum price cap, and the home needs few repairs or the seller is willing to make all the repairs before closing, then this is probably the way for you to go.

Sub-prime: A loan that is not as valuable to a lender as a prime. A person with a low credit score would be considered sub-prime, and will have to pay a higher interest rate for this loan to help outweigh the risks the creditor is taking.

CONVENTIONAL LOANS

Conventional loans are neither FHA nor VA loans. They are not insured by any government agency. They are loans that your bank, mortgage company, or credit union make to you. The lending institutions get the money to loan from investors, and the loans are uninsured if you have the right credit score and down payment. If your down payment is less than 20 percent, the loans are usually insured by a private company, with a fee that you pay monthly called PMI.

Conventional loans are available to anyone who is a U.S. citizen, resident alien, or is working under an acceptable work visa. Some conventional loans allow exceptions to this, but they would be

GEEKOID

Who are Freddie Mac and Fannie Mae? Freddie Mac is the Federal Home Loan Mortgage Corporation (FHLMC) and Fannie Mae is the Federal National Mortgage Association (FNMA). They are secondary market lenders. They make money from investors more easily available to lenders for conventional loans.

considered non-conforming or sub-prime, and each case would be handled separately. Conventional loans can sometimes offer programs for people with other special circumstances, such as self-employed individuals who do not want to have to show proof of income. In this instance, the borrower would have to have a high credit score and a big down payment. Ask your lender about other special programs that may fit your circumstances.

GEEK GLOSSARY

PITI is an acronym for Principal, Interest, Taxes, and Insurance. This is your total mortgage payment after adding taxes and homeowner's insurance.

Conventional loans are broken down into two categories, conforming and non-conforming. Conforming loans have terms and conditions that follow guidelines set out by Fannie Mae and Freddie Mac. These are secondary lenders that purchase mortgages from the institutions that lend to you. They set limits on the amount of any mortgage they will purchase from lenders. Currently, the maximum loan amount for a conforming loan is $417,000 for the forty-eight states and Washington D.C.; $625,000 in Alaska and Hawaii.

Loans that exceed the amount for conforming loans are called jumbo or non-conforming loans. Because jumbo loans create more risk, they typically require a larger down payment, carry a higher interest rate, and may include extra underwriting restrictions as well.

GUERRILLA GEEK

When comparing two offers, one with a conventional loan and one with a VA or FHA loan, the seller will almost always choose the conventional because its fees are lower.

Maximum Purchase Price	The maximum purchase price for a conforming conventional loan is currently $417,000, but is updated on an annual basis. Anything above that amount is considered a jumbo, or non-conforming, conventional loan.
Minimum Down Payment	Down payments range from 0 to 20%. The lower your down payment, the higher your interest rate and mortgage insurance. Higher credit scores are also required for lower down payments, as are higher cash reserves.
Debt-to-Income Ratios	Mortgage payment (PITI) should not exceed 33% of gross monthly income. Combined debts (PITI, car payments, credit cards) should not exceed 41% of gross monthly income. Car payments and other installment debts with more than 10 months remaining and all credit card debt is included. Non-conforming and sub-prime loans may not require any income to debt documentation, depending on credit score and down payment.
Interest Rate	Interest rate will depend upon your credit score, but the rate is generally the same for FHA, VA, and conventional conforming loans. The interest rate is higher for jumbo or other non-conforming loans, such as sub-prime.
Mortgage Insurance	Mortgage insurance for conventional loans is called PMI (private mortgage insurance). The rates vary, and mainly depend on the amount of your down payment. For example, if you pay zero down, your PMI might be 1.5% of your monthly payment. If you pay 10% down, that would decrease to .75% of your monthly payment. If you pay 20% or more down, there is no PMI required. Note that if you have PMI at the beginning of your loan, you can usually have it removed after you have made enough payments to pay your loan down to less than 80% of your original purchase price. Be careful about this though; it's not always as easy to do as your mortgage person tells you, and depending on the investor, they may actually require your balance to be as low as 70% of the original purchase price.
Credit Score Requirements	Conventional loans generally require a higher credit score than VA or FHA loans. The minimum credit score varies greatly, depending on amount of down payment, your reserves, and your income. For example, if you have a low credit score, but recently graduated med school, you can get a loan easily. Or if you have a low credit score but recently became an heir to lots of money, you could get a loan easily. However, for the average person it's best to have a credit score of at least 620.
Seller Contributions	The seller can contribute a portion of or all of the buyer's closing costs and pre-paids. The seller can pay up to 3% of the sales price toward the borrower's costs when the down payment is 0 – 5%. The seller can pay up to 6% of the sales price when the down payment is 10% or greater.

Borrowed Funds	A buyer may borrow all funds needed for down payment, closing, and pre-paid costs as long as they are borrowed against an asset of the borrower, such as 401(k), stocks, bonds, or other real estate. Second liens may also be used to borrow funds for a down payment, which is sometimes the best option to avoid mortgage insurance premiums.
Gifts	Gifts for funds for down payment, closing costs, and prepaids may be obtained from a relative or someone with a defined relationship, as long as the borrower demonstrates that 5% of funds needed are from their own resources, such as borrowed funds or cash. Exceptions are sometimes made for the relationship rule.

Mortgage Terms

Mortgages are available for different terms, but the most popular mortgage is the thirty-year mortgage. The next most popular is the fifteen-year, but you can also go as long as forty years, or five, ten, or twenty years. Generally, a forty-year mortgage will carry a higher interest rate than a thirty-year mortgage, and a thirty-year mortgage will have a higher interest rate than a fifteen-year mortgage. When you get into the other terms, the interest rate may not go lower with

GEEKOID

You may be able to eliminate PMI with the use of second lien financing. You can close on the second lien at the same time as the first, and borrow your down payment. This interest is then tax deductible, and most people pay off their second mortgage much more quickly than the first, eventually giving you more equity in your home.

If you have a 5 percent down payment, you can borrow the other 15 percent, making your first mortgage 80 percent, with no PMI.

the term. They will give you a twenty-year mortgage: you just may not get a rate break from a thirty-year due to the fact that it's not a high-demand product.

Fixed Rates

With a fixed-rate mortgage, your payments will be constant for

"Fixed" is the operative word in a fixed rate home mortgage. You have a fixed rate of interest over a fixed period of time.

the entire life of the loan. The payments are calculated to pay off the mortgage balance at the end of the term. The most common terms are fifteen and thirty years, although some lenders even offer terms of twenty, twenty-five, and even forty years. Just remember that the longer the term, the more interest you'll pay.

A fixed rate offers the obvious benefit of stability. You know that your mortgage payments will be the same each year, which will make it easier to budget, knowing that the amount will not change.

GUERRILLA GEEK

By the time you finish paying off the mortgage on your home, you'll have paid more in interest alone than the actual purchase price of the house. With that in mind, it just makes sense to shop around for the best interest rate available.

Adjustable Rate Mortgages (ARMs)

Until the early 1980s, almost all mortgages had a fixed rate, with the borrower knowing exactly what he or she would be paying each month for the next thirty years. But when interest rates began to go higher and higher, lenders realized that they were losing money by being locked into one rate for the term of the mortgage.

Adjustable rate mortgages were born from this dilemma. They feature interest rates that may change over time, causing your

GEEKOID

Many ARMs offer caps on the interest rate, that is, the amount that the interest rate can increase is "capped." The cap is typically 4 to 6 percent above the current market interest rate.

GUERRILLA GEEK

Although interest rates changes with ARMs, consumers are protected by limits, or caps, on how much rates can increase. There are two types of interest rate caps. **Periodic caps** limit the amount your interest rate can increase from one adjustment period to the next. You should be aware that now all ARMs have periodic rate caps. **Overall caps** limit how much the interest rate can increase over the life of the loan. Overall caps have been required by law since 1987.

Here are some other terms that you should know: **balloon** and **interest-only mortgages**. Balloon notes are mortgages that are due in full after a predetermined period. A five-year balloon note is due in full after five years. This is not a good product for most people. An interest-only mortgage is just what its name implies—your payment is calculated on interest only, giving you a lower payment for more house. What's the catch? You owe the same balance thirty years from now—this is never a good idea. If you can only afford an interest-only loan, you're spending too much and could end up losing everything.

payment to increase or decrease as a result. These loans typically have an initial fixed rate lower than that of a comparable fixed rate mortgage. Then the initial fixed rate period is followed by adjustment intervals. For instance, you might start at a relatively low rate for the first three years; then an adjustment would be made in your rate. It would be adjusted again at period intervals.

Because ARMs offer lower rates initially, they have become popular and effective ways to help prospective homebuyers become homeowners during times of high interest rates. But because payments and interest rates can increase, homebuyers considering this type of mortgage need to be certain that their income will be able to keep up with the changes.

Another consideration is that not only can the interest rate change, it can change frequently over the life of the loan. Some ARMs are structured so that interest rates can nearly double in just a few years.

You can shop and compare ARMs against fixed-rate loans if you know the terms. The first number indicates the length of the initial period. The second number indicates how often the rate is adjusted. For example, a 3/1 ARM means that your interest rate stays the same for three years, then adjusts each year. It's important to know when it will adjust, and what the cap is. If an adjustable rate goes too high, you can refinance to a fixed-rate loan, but that could cost you a lot of money.

Adjustable rate mortgages are usually a good option for someone who knows they will be in a particular house for a short period of time, like less than three years.

GEEK AT A GLANCE

- Deciding which mortgage is right for you should not be difficult. You may choose from FHA, VA, or conventional loans.

- FHA and VA loans are not issued directly from government agencies, but they are insured by them.

- Different types of loans have specific qualification requirements. Check each to see if you qualify. For example, VA loans are available only to active and discharged veterans. Eligibility certificates are required for application.

- Each type of loan will have other restrictions as well, such as limits on the amount of money available.

HOMING IN ON HOMING OPTIONS

Once you've got your money matters organized, you'll have to decide what you'll spend that money on. It will help to know what types of homes are available.

There are three basic types of home ownership from which you will choose. This chapter will explain the difference in them, and how each will differ in your payment and other expenses, such as maintenance.

Types of Homes

The three types of home ownership are fee simple (also called freehold), which are single-family homes, sometimes attached multi-family homes, such as duplexes and town homes; condominiums; and co-operatives (called co-ops for short).

GEEKOID

As you begin your search, it's a good idea to keep a notebook for comments about each house you see. Before you begin to see houses, make a list of general attributes you're looking for, and then as you go through each house, note on the chart how each house measures up for every item.

GUERRILLA GEEK

Planned Unit Development, or PUD, is a type of ownership where your home is one of many homes in a defined community, which may include detached single-family homes, town houses, apartments, or condominiums. You control your home or unit, and have community rights to facilities such as parking, swimming pool, playground, and community center or club house. The community association has control over the common areas and charges a monthly, quarterly, or annual fee for their upkeep. You usually have the right to be a part of the association board that makes the decisions about what the fees to the owners will be and how that money will be used.

Some community or homeowner associations are voluntary, but if your home is a PUD, the homeowner's dues are mandatory.

Fee Simple

Most detached, single-family homes are owned fee simple. This means that you own the house, the yard, and anything else that is on your property. You can do anything you want to your house once you own it, including painting the exterior any color you choose, and building anything on your lot, like a fence or swimming pool. You can build onto your house as your space allows, and the only restrictions to consider are any local zoning requirements or any restricting covenants that might affect the property.

GEEKOID

Taking photos of the houses you see is a good idea to help you remember and sort all your options. Check with the current homeowner first to be sure that he or she does not mind the picture taking.

Of course, with ownership comes responsibility, so you have to provide insurance for your entire house, including liability insurance for the property. And you are solely responsible for repairs and routine maintenance that might be needed.

 Sometimes your price range and market you are looking in will decide your ownership type or home style for you. Knowing the facts before you go in will help you be better prepared for all the choices you will have.

Single-family Homes. Sometimes referred to as detached single family homes, these are what most people refer to as houses. Since they are the most common type of residence, here are a few types of house styles to help you learn the lingo for your search. These terms sometimes vary in different parts of the country, but most MLS systems use them in their descriptions.

• One-level, ranch, rancher, or rambler. This is a one-level house, meaning all of the living space is on one level. A one-level house sometimes has a basement.

• Garden or patio home. Many of the one-level houses built after 1990 are referred to as garden homes, but a house is technically a garden home if the outside walls touch the property line. A lot of people are drawn to these homes because you get the convenience of a single family home, but with minimum lawn maintenance. These are also called patio homes.

A Sears house is an owner-built house that was sold by Sears, Roebuck and Co. through its catalog division from 1904 to 1940. You could order a kit, and it would be sent to you through the mail. No kidding.

• A-frame – This was a popular house style in the 1970s, and is in the shape of an A. They are usually built of cedar or other natural wood.

• Cape Cod – These homes are popular in the northeast, but can be found in most parts of the country. This architectural style has recognizable dormers on the second floor. It usually has one bedroom down and two bedrooms up.

• Cottage – A cottage is usually a small one-level house. A lot of cottages are one or two bedrooms, usually with one bath. The term cottage often means that a house is charming and cozy, sometimes built of traditional materials like stone or brick. Most have a garden in the front or back.

• Colonial – This style is usually a two- or three-story house, sometimes with a basement. The traditional floor plan usually has living areas on the first floor and bedrooms upstairs. This is one of the most popular floor plans in America, due to the sensible layout, and the division of living space from the bedrooms. It generally brings the best resale value, compared with split level or split foyer homes. One drawback is that the master

A **starter home** is a small, inexpensive home usually appropriate for first-time homebuyers.

bedroom is usually upstairs with all other bedrooms, and buyers are now trending toward wanting the master on the main level, or away from the other bedrooms. This style may include a one- or two-car garage.

• Split Level – A split level house has three levels. Most have a living room, kitchen, and dining room on the main or entry level, with the bedrooms upstairs and a den and/or garage downstairs from the main level. In the northeast, some have a basement downstairs from

Famous split level homes: The Bradys of the infamous *Brady Bunch* lived in a split level home, and the Keatons on *Family Ties* lived in a split level.

the den/garage area. Split level homes provide a lot of space for the money, and a lot of people like having the bedrooms separate from the living area.

• Split Foyer – In a split foyer home, there is a landing for the foyer, and then stairs going up to the bedrooms, living room, kitchen, and dining room, and stairs going down to a den and usually a garage. This is an economical floor plan, but is not as popular for resale. These floor plans generally bring less resale value than colonial, one-level, or split level homes. This floor plan is called a raised ranch in some parts of the country.

• Town House – The term town house usually refers to an attached dwelling, meaning that there are several units in one building. A town house usually has two or three stories, and shares one or both sides with another unit.

GUERRILLA GEEK

McMansion is a slang architectural term which first came into use during the 1980s as a pejorative description and an idiom. It describes a particular style of housing that—as its name suggests—is large like a mansion and as ubiquitous as McDonald's restaurants. The same criticisms that have been levied at the restaurants have been attached to these houses that share their name: a deviation from style of other houses nearby, a mass-produced appearance, and a perceived negative impact on nature and neighbors. Slang terms have been created to express disapproval of these houses: "Beltway Baronial," "Starter Castle," "Tract Mansion, and "Faux-chateau" are just a few of the most common.

- Row House – A row house is similar to a town house, and is a popular style of housing in Baltimore, Philadelphia, San Francisco, and Washington, D.C. The houses are attached on one or both sides, and they are

Rowhouses line Philadelphia's Elfreth's Alley, the oldest continuously occupied road in America.

situated in rows. They are usually deep and narrow.

Here is a summary of advantages and disadvantages of fee simple homes:

Advantages
- Your home is your own. You can put nails in walls, or modify it any way you want. You can even add extra rooms since it's yours.
- Re-sale value is generally the highest of all housing types.
- There is usually no other management but you, and no management fees. Some single-family homes are part of a home owner's association, but those fees are usually minimal.

GEEKOID

Some town homes or row homes are owned as attached single-family home units (fee simple), and some are owned as condominiums. If you're interested in a particular town home, be sure to confirm the type of ownership with your agent or the seller. Ask to see the tax record to confirm that this information is correct.

GEEKOID

If you buy a condominium, be sure to check for bylaws, covenants, and regulations that come with it. You may be restricted about pets, parking, and even what's allowed to be displayed on the front of your home such as blinds and curtains.

Disadvantages
- All maintenance and repair costs must be borne by you.
- You must provide all insurance.
- There may be no amenities such as a pool or playground that are found in other housing types.
- Single unit homes are usually more expensive than condos or co-ops.

GUERRILLA GEEK

Studies show that first-time homebuyers are likely to buy attached homes, such as condos and town homes. Repeat buyers more often buy detached, single-family homes.

CONDOMINIUMS

In a condo, you usually own the inside of your unit (from the inside walls in), and the outside walls, roof, and other outdoor facilities are owned in common, meaning you share ownership of those with the other residents. You have to pay a monthly fee to maintain these areas. This fee usually covers liability insurance for the common areas and maintenance on the building's exterior. So if the building needs a new roof or exterior painting, that will come out of your fees, not out of your savings account.

Most attached, multi-family building units are owned as condominiums, and some detached single family houses are as well. This means that you own your unit or house, and have certain rights to the common areas, such as parking, swimming pools, or club house.

Here are the pros and cons of condominiums:

Advantages

- You are responsible for little or no maintenance.
- Amenities such as pools and recreational areas are often available.
- Condominiums are often located near shopping and work areas.
- This type of housing is often more affordable than single unit houses.

Disadvantages

- Association membership fees may apply.
- There is usually less privacy than with a single unit home.
- You only own from your interior walls inward. The rest of the structure and all the land is commonly owned.
- Some condos take longer to sell than other forms of housing.

GEEKOID

More and more single-family homes are owned as condominiums, especially in retirement communities. This offers the privacy of a single-family home, but with none of the upkeep. Most of these new condominium associations even cut your grass for you.

CO-OPS

This type of ownership is more common in large cities, such as New York or Washington, D.C. It is similar to condominium ownership, except that instead of owning your unit, you own a percentage of shares in the entire building or complex. In other words, you own a share in a corporation that owns the building and all units, and you have rights to a specific unit.

Co-ops are managed by a co-op board, which has control over almost every aspect of the units, such as who can live there, what renovations can be done, and even whether or not pets are allowed. You usually pay a monthly fee that includes your mortgage and all maintenance fees for the building. One thing co-op boards are notorious for is screening buyers, meaning you could secure a nice sale when you're ready to move, and without their approval, you will lose the sale.

Here are the advantages and disadvantages of this type of home:

Advantages
- Since there is joint-ownership, there is a sense of community.
- Management is by an elected committee, with specific committees handling maintenance, finance, and social events.

Disadvantages
- You only own shares in your home, not your home.
- Since the home is not yours, you have less authority over it.

- The three types of home ownership are fee simple, condominium, and co-operative.

- The primary types of homes available are detached single unit homes, attached multiple-unit homes, and co-ops.

- Each type has advantages and disadvantages that should be investigated before buying.

DECIDING ON YOUR DWELLING

Now that you know the general types of housing available, think about the features you want in a home, and decide which type is right for you.

Make a list of features you want, and those you don't want, and add to it as you have time to consider your options. Here are some questions to ask yourself as your list takes shape.

- Do you know the three most important things to consider when buying a home? Location, location, location! Yes, they're all the same thing, but it's such an important factor, it bears repeating. If you haven't heard this before, get used to hearing it now. It's a popular phrase among house hunters and sellers.

GUERRILLA GEEK

Beware of a community that has too many homes for sale. There could be a big and undesirable change coming to the area that your research hasn't turned up.

You can change a lot of things about a house, but location isn't one of them. Consider places you'd like to be near, like work, school, church, and other important activities.

Are there undesirable places you want to avoid, like industrial or shopping areas? Here are some other factors that make location critical:

- Tax rate – Will you pay only city taxes, or city and county?

- Zoning – Even if there's nothing objectionable nearby now, could zoning allow for something undesirable in the future?
- Noise – Is the location peaceful?
- Crime – What is the crime rate?
- City/County services – Will you have fire department and law enforcement coverage?
- Restrictive covenants – Will you be allowed to add extras you might want?
- Neighbors – Do they have similar values?

• Are you handy enough with a hammer to take on a fixer-upper that may save you money, or would you prefer something that's in perfect shape already?

• How much closet space will you need? How much other storage space?

• Should your home be one, two, or more levels? In other words, are stairs a problem? If not now, will you live there long enough so that they become a problem as you age? You should also consider the needs of frequent guests, such as your parents.

• Do you mind keeping up a yard, or is just a token patch of grass enough for you? Keep in mind, too, that all that equipment you may need translates into extra expenses.

GEEKOID

One way to learn what kind of neighbors you'd have in a particular location is to drive by the neighborhood at night or on the weekend and see what's going on. If there's a neighborhood meeting, attend and ask questions.

- Do you want to own land in addition to the actual home? Are trees in the yard important?

- How many bathrooms must you have?

- How many bedrooms do you need, and how should they be situated? Should they all be on one level together, or do you want the master bedroom separated from the others?

- If you enjoy entertaining, what kind of area will you need for that?

- Is a pool essential? This probably shouldn't be a deal breaker. If you can't find a home that already has a nice pool, at least find one with a good place to install one later.

GEEK*Speak:*

"I always thought a yard was three feet, then I started mowing the lawn."

C.E. Cowman

Before you buy a house thinking you'll remodel it to make it your dream, check local zoning laws to be sure your changes will be allowed.

- Are there critical needs to consider, such as proximity to medical care?

- Are the utilities you want available? Some communities do not have natural gas, meaning you will be forced to use electric appliances, such as hot water heaters, central heating, and stoves.

A **basement** is a part of a house that is fully or partially underground, usually directly beneath the living area. A garage is a covered and enclosed parking area that is often built into a house's roofline. A **garage** has a door to fully enclose the area after the car has been pulled in or out of the parking area. They are wonderful if you live in an area where you have to scrape ice or snow from the windshield, or where your car would get baked in the sun with no protection.

- Do you need a basement or garage?

- What type of material do you want on the outside of the house—brick, vinyl, or something painted (which means the effort and expense to keep it looking nice!)?

- What type of neighborhood suits you—a sprawling bedroom community, or something in the middle of the hustle and bustle of the city?

GEEKOID

When you've identified a place you like, take time to drive by and observe what goes on at different times of day. Will school traffic block your driveway at certain times? Do parked cars from a nearby park overflow onto your street when there's a big game?

- Are you basically a formal or informal person? Particular stylistic preferences might influence your choice of a home.

- Does your family life center around the kitchen? If so, you'll want a big one. Don't worry about appliances—those can be replaced. Just look at the space and how it's situated.

- Do you love a bright, sunny room lit by natural sunlight? If so, windows will be important to you.

GEEK*Speak:*

"Houses are built to live in, and not to look on: therefore let use be preferred before uniformity."

Francis Bacon

- What about aesthetics and extras like an office/library, sewing room, or laundry room?

- Are there special considerations you want to avoid? For instance, if some homes in your target area are in a flood zone, you will certainly want to know that and avoid them.

GEEKOID

Identifying from the start what features are must-haves and which are negotiable can help you know which houses you'll want to take the time to see. It will also keep you from wasting time looking at the ones that don't fit the bill.

GEEK AT A GLANCE

- Make a list of features that you would like in a house and add to it as you think of more.

- Location is probably the most important factor in looking for a house. Look for the obvious, like what's next to the house you are considering, but also consider intangibles like zoning laws and tax rates.

- Serious consideration of your list of important factors will help you decide what housing situation is best for you.

UNDERSTANDING THE ROLE OF AGENTS

Buying a home is typically the most significant financial undertaking in a person's life. That's why it is important to consider whether you are qualified to represent yourself in this situation, or if you feel that it is necessary to have a professional represent you.

In the days before computers, MLS (Multiple Listing System) books were only being printed once or twice a month. Other than just driving around and stumbling upon a house you liked, contacting an agent to gain access to the MLS was almost the only comprehensive way to see all the homes for sale in a particular area.

Today, with the use of the Internet, home buyers have access to MLS information almost as soon as the agents themselves. Even people selling without an agent can have their homes posted on the web for the world to see.

GEEK GLOSSARY

Multiple Listing Service (MLS) is a database that allows real estate agents and brokers to share information about available properties. Its purpose is to provide a source of information about all homes available within a given area or price range. Most MLS systems limit access to agents and brokers who are properly licensed by the state.

Even though this change has made it possible to locate homes for sale without professional help, an agent can give you advice and information beyond the facts you need about finding your home. Besides information about which neighborhood is in your price range, and which have had historically higher appreciation over time, you are often able to get more facts like information on the school system, zoning changes that affect buyers, and other important information.

If this is your first time to buy a house, you should definitely consider having an agent represent you. Why? Because it will often cost you nothing in fees, and it could save you thousands of dollars and a lot of heartache. But you should understand the role that agents play in selling and buying homes, whether you plan to use one or not. Otherwise you're moving around in the market blindly.

When looking for a home you can either go it alone or have representation by signing with a buyer's agent.

> ## GEEKOID
>
> How are agents paid? Most agents work on a certain percentage of the home's sale price, paid by the seller at closing. This is usually 6 to 7 percent, but this is always negotiable between the agent and his or her client. Buyer's agents work in the same manner, with agents for the buyer and the seller splitting the commission.

- You can go it alone, and follow up leads and ads you may be interested in, as well as checking out new houses being built.

- You can call the listing agent for each home you want to see and ask him or her to show you the homes. This may also be seen as going it alone because you haven't committed to having an agent of your own to help you.

GUERRILLA GEEK

All real estate licenses are not the same. Only real estate licensees who are members of the National Association of REALTORS® are properly called REALTORS®. Agents with this designation subscribe to a strict code of ethics and are expected to command a higher level of knowledge about the real estate process.

- You can sign a contract with a buyer's agent, having that agent show you everything you want to see.

Let's take a look at what you can expect from each of these options.

Going it Alone

Many people try to find a home without professional help because they are trying to keep from paying someone to help them. If you decide to look for a home without the help of an agent, this means that you'll be responsible for finding available houses, arranging to see them, and negotiating and closing the deal yourself. If you find a home offered for sale through an agent, the agent will be working for the seller.

GEEK GLOSSARY

FSBO stands for For Sale By Owner. It refers to property being sold by the owner without any help from a real estate agent.

GUERRILLA GEEK

If you plan to find a home all on your on, look into the various web sites that list homes for sale by owner. Salebyowner.com and Forsalebyowner.com are two examples of sites that will allow you to search for homes in your area. Owner contact information is provided so you can get additional information or schedule an appointment.

There are definite advantages to working solo. For one thing, you are in complete control of the process. You see only the houses you want to see, with no pressure to waste time on those that are close to your ideal, but really aren't what you had in mind. That means, too, that you can work at your own pace. If things develop to make you want to hasten or slow the process, you are free to do so without consulting anyone. For better or worse, you are your own representative.

There are disadvantages, too. Your choices will be limited, and you will not have the benefit of an experienced hand in looking for the right house or negotiating for it. You will also have no one to help tie up all the loose ends of

REALTOR® is a two-syllable word. It is not pronounced real-a-tor. Most people pronounce it incorrectly, so if you say it incorrectly, the error will either go unnoticed, or others will begin to say it like you because they don't know any better.

closing. Also, since you'll be your own representative, you'll have to meet face-to-face with the sellers or their agents—there will be no buffer if things get sticky. What should be an objective process will be subjective.

A recent study found that 85 percent of homebuyers surveyed relied on real estate professionals to help them in their search for their new home.

Calling the Listing Agent

More people, however, decide to get help in finding their dream home. They find a house they want to see, get the name of the agent that has it listed, and give them a call to see the house.

The agent who listed the house is called the listing agent. If it is sold by another agent, the selling agent, the commission for the sale is split between the two.

This encourages other agents representing buyers to show their home. This commission is paid out of the proceeds of the home

A Comparable Market Analysis (CMA) shows what properties similar to the one you are considering have sold for within a recent period of time. Be sure to note that it is not the listing prices that are provided in this report, but the amount for which they actually sold. This document can help you determine the price you can expect to pay.

GEEKOID

Buyers' agents often include the designation ABR after their names. This stands for Accredited Buyer Representative and is used by agents who specialize in helping buyers find their dream home. EBA is another designation for buyer's agents, which stands for Exclusive Buyer Agent. It is used for agents that never represent sellers. Agents must complete educational courses and represent a certain number of buyers to earn those designations.

when it sells. At closing, the listing agent gets his or her portion of the fee, and the selling agent gets his or her portion.

That means that if the company that has a home listed has two thousand agents working for them, all two thousand agents represent the seller. When a real estate agent lists a house, the listing belongs to the company, not the agent. This may be TMI, but it is essential to know. When you call a listing agent to show you a house, they can handle all the paperwork for you, but they cannot give you advice, and they cannot give you any information that would hurt the seller or bring the seller a lower price.

To fully appreciate how that will impact you as the buyer, let's take a look at the things the agent will not be able to reveal to you.

- The reason the property is being sold, unless the seller specifically releases that information

- Any concessions the seller might be willing to make

- The substance of conversations between the seller and the agent

GEEKOID

When using a buyer's agent, you should never contact a listing agent or owner directly without informing them right away that you have a buyer's agent. This is unethical, and could get you into a sticky situation. If your agent is out of town, they will usually have a partner that you can work with to keep the wheels rolling. If you see a home that you just can't wait to see, and you do contact the listing agent or owner, just tell them that you have an agent, that you can't get in touch with him or her, but would like to see the home. Let them know that your agent will then be following up if you decide to make an offer. Otherwise, you could end up owing a commission to the listing agent and to your agent.

- Any information that could give you, the buyer, an advantage, including a Comparable Market Analysis (CMA) that could put the seller at a disadvantage.

GUERRILLA GEEK

If you're working with an agent, they will often give you copies of the printout from the MLS system in your area. These vary from region to region, but generally include the same basic information.

GEEKOID

A buyer's agent can offer you a comparative market analysis (CMA) of any house you're interested in that will show you what similar properties sold for in that same neighborhood. No doubt the seller's agent has done the same to help them settle on a price, but they may have added something to it to allow for negotiation or profit.

• Even if the selling agent knows that the house is overpriced by $30,000, he or she cannot tell you that.

Getting a Buyer's Agent

GEEKOID

Buyer's agents sometimes charge a flat or even an hourly fee, but usually they simply split the commission paid by the seller for the sale of the property.

Just like a seller of a house contracts with an agent to list his or her home, you can establish a contract with a buyer's agent to act on your behalf. This agreement makes the agent accountable to you.

A buyer's agent's job is to represent you, give you advice and counsel, and make sure you get the best deal possible. They expect to get paid for representing you, but their fee almost always comes from the seller, not from you, meaning you get free service. If you decide to use a buyer's agent, discuss with them up front how they would be paid and whether or not you would have to pay anything.

A qualified real estate agent in any market can show you any house listed in the MLS. This saves you time, because you choose

GUERRILLA GEEK

In 1983, a Federal Trade Commission study revealed that over 72 percent of home buyers erroneously believed that they were being represented by agents showing them homes. As a result, laws have been passed to assure that agents disclose exactly who they represent. The concept of buyer's agents began to develop in an effort to have buyers represented as well as sellers.

one agent, you tell them where you are looking and your price range, and they can show you every house listed that meets your criteria.

The MLS listing should also show the fee paid by the seller to the agent that sells that house. They can also search for specific features you require, such as number of bedrooms, number of baths, fireplace, basement, garage, or any other features you want or need. They can set up appointments and show you all the properties back to back, rather than you having to call each listing agent and see each property separately.

A buyer's agent will work to negotiate the best price for you, ensuring that the property is inspected, and will make sure that you are fully represented in all aspects of the sale. Since he or she is looking out for your best interest, you will be able to see not only homes listed in the Multiple Listing Service, but also homes that are for sale by owner, as well as homes under construction by builders.

The most basic thing to know is that you should choose an agent that is different from the one the seller is using. Using the same agent

GUERRILLA GEEK

Keep in mind that if you have been working with a buyer's agent and buy a home that is for sale by owner, the buyer's agent is still owed a commission. Most serious, informed sellers know this, and have usually built this fee into their asking price. If not, they may still be willing to pay it if you ask. However, it sometimes happens that a seller won't budge, and you will have to pay this fee.

You should discuss this situation with your agent upfront, and ask what their fee is for this. Sometimes they will charge a reduced fee, such as 2 or 2-1/2 percent. You should decide going in if you are willing to pay the fee. If not, do not waste an agent's time. It is not fair to ask someone to work for months for you, and then buy a home without their getting paid. A lot of buyers will do this without ever telling their agent—it's just not an ethical thing to do, and it could hurt you in the end as well.

to represent you would be like having the same attorney represent both sides in a court case. It will benefit you as a buyer to have someone on your side that is obliged to negotiate in your best interest, to not disclose confidential information about you as the buyer, and to reveal to you all pertinent factors affecting the value of the property.

Here are some things a buyer's agent can provide for you:

- Reasons the property is being sold

- Potential concessions by the seller, or other information that may work to your advantage

- Relevant information about property value trends

- A CMA analysis revealing asking and closing prices on similar properties in the area

After finding a home you like, the buyer's agent can pull comps on other houses that have sold recently, to help you decide if the house is priced right. They can also offer advice on what you should offer, and what might be too much to pay. Then they do all the negotiation, which takes a lot of stress off you. Having a professional negotiator is almost always better in getting you the best price.

GEEKOID

Going to an open house may seem like a good idea, but if you are working with an agent or broker, check with him or her first. He or she may want to go with you, or at the very least, may want to send a business card for you to give the agent hosting the event. This will send a clear signal that you are already represented in your search and can prevent misunderstandings later.

Types of Agencies

As you begin to look for an agent, there are some important terms that affect the job the agent can do for you. Here are some you should know:

- Subagency: This type of agency is not typically allowed in the U.S. these days. Anyone other than the listing agent showing a home used to be referred to as a subagent. Not only could they show the home, they could actually advertise it and put their sign in the yard. This was confusing to consumers.

- Single Agency: As implied, this means that an agent represents a single person, either the seller or the buyer. The seller's agent works for the seller only and is also referred to as the listing agent. When an agent works as a seller's agent, the agent has a

GUERRILLA GEEK

It is probably not surprising that in our age of electronics, there would be virtual real estate agents to help you in your search for a home. At sites offering this type of help, you can get the services of an actual agent with lower commission fees offered to sellers and rebates for buyers. They also provide the buyer with search tools and a tracking system to keep up with homes under consideration, plus help from live agents in your area if you need it.

fiduciary duty to the seller. A fiduciary relationship is one that is founded in trust and implies that an agent owes his/her client loyalty, confidentiality, loyalty, disclosure, diligence, obedience, accounting, and reasonable care. A buyer's agent works for the buyer only and is sometimes called the selling agent.

- Dual Agency: This is also known as limited consensual dual agency. One party represents both the seller and the buyer which can only be done with prior written consent of both parties. As previously mentioned, this is not a good idea. In this arrangement, the agent is limited in what they can do for both the buyer and seller. The agent may not tell the seller if the buyer is willing to pay more than their offer unless the buyer gives the agent specific permission. The agent also may not tell the buyer that the seller is willing to accept an offer lower than the list price unless given specific permission by the seller. The agent has the same fiduciary relationship to both the buyer and seller to disclose any "material fact," which would be any fact that may make you change your mind about buying or selling. They must also disclose any misrepresentation or fraud. Dual agency comes about if a buyer has an agent, and they decide to buy a house that their agent has listed. It sometimes happens, and dual agency is entered before going to contract.

- Transaction Broker: He or she assists one or more parties who are customers in a sale. He or she provides limited representation, including dealing honestly and fairly; accounts for all funds; uses skill, care, and diligence in dealing with the customer; and discloses all facts that materially affect the value of residential property but that are not readily observed by the buyer. Additional duties may be entered into the written agreement. If you call a listing agent and want him or her to handle your paperwork but not represent you, they become your transition broker.

GEEK AT A GLANCE

- You must decide whether you will search for your house alone, call agents that have houses listed for sellers and FSBOs, or whether you will enlist an agent to work for you.

- The most important thing to know here is that when you call an agent to show you a house he or she has listed, that agent is working for the seller, as are the other agents in his or her agency.

- An agent working for the seller is not obliged to tell you why the property is being sold, about any concessions the seller might be willing to make to seal the deal, or even if the house is overpriced.

- A buyer's agent works for the buyer and is able to provide pertinent information to help the buyer make a wise choice.

SIGNING WITH AN AGENT

Once you decide to use an agent, how do you go about finding the right one?

Your search for the right agent really has two parts. The first thing you'll need to know is where to get the names of qualified and experienced agents. The second thing to know is what qualities you should be looking for so you can select the right person from all those that are available. Here's help with both of those processes.

Where to Look for an Agent

There are some really good places to look for an agent to help you. One is bound to put you in touch with the right person.

- Personal referrals – This is probably the best way to find a good agent. Ask your friends and acquaintances to recommend someone who has been of help to them, and what the agent's strengths and weaknesses are. Mention the things that are important to you, and ask how the agent handled those issues.

GEEKOID

When choosing an agent, do not be pressured into using someone just because they are related, or are the friend of a friend. Buying a home is too big a thing to trust with someone you would not have chosen on your own.

GEEKOID

Here's a breakdown from the national Association of REALTORS® that shows how most people find a real estate agent:

- Referred by friend, neighbor, or relative – 40 percent
- Used the agent previously – 13 percent
- Met the agent at an open house – 7 percent
- Signed with the agent on duty at the office – 4 percent
- Found on the Internet – 7 percent

- Internet – This can be an invaluable tool in your search for an agent. Many real estate agencies whose names you obtained from yard signs have web sites that you can browse and see who is available to help you. Some sites even offer the chance to chat anonymously with agents in a cyber-interview before you make a commitment to anyone in particular. Do they appear to be representing their sellers well? If so, they would probably represent you well, too.

GUERRILLA GEEK

Even if you're looking for a home in another city, a local agency can recommend someone to use in your new location. Ask if they have a relocation department, which can be helpful in your move.

- Advertisements – No doubt you often get ads for various agents in your mailbox. If you see someone that looks interesting, follow up that lead. Look in the yellow pages, too. There are plenty of ads for agencies and agents in the real estate section.

  Also, if your neighborhood is like most others, there are always lots of signs displaying names of real estate companies and agents. You can get some idea of who lists a lot of houses by noting the names you see frequently.

- Cold calling – If all those sources fail, try calling several local agencies and ask to speak with someone available to help you. This probably isn't the best way to find an agent, but you may get lucky and get connected to someone eager to prove him or herself.

What to Look for in an Agent

Once you get the names of several good candidates, you should schedule appointments with each one, meet with him or her, and decide which one you want to work with. Here are some particular things you'll want to look for:

GEEKOID

HomeGain is the name of a website that can help locate the right agent for you. You submit a profile about the home you want to buy or sell, and the site notifies agents near you, who submit proposals for your needs. Then you choose the agent you prefer based on what they've submitted.

GEEKOID

When choosing an agent, a good rule of thumb is to look for someone with at least two years of experience. He or she has probably learned the fundamentals by then, and has handled enough transactions to be able to guide you through the experience.

- Experience – If this is your first home, you will want someone experienced to answer your questions and help you through the maze of decisions. If you're a veteran of home buying, you won't need as much help, and you may prefer a go-getter just starting out.

Newcomers to the field may offer enthusiasm and availability of time. They may be willing to go the extra mile to make a sale critical to the start of their career. You may be offered more one-on-one time with a rookie. And they may be more willing to listen to your opinions and preferences.

GEEKOID

An independent survey reports that 84 percent of home buyers would use the same real estate agent again.

There is something to be said for experience as well. After all, this is one of the biggest purchases you will ever make. However, the seasoned pro in the office may be in such demand that you are assigned to one of his or her assistants, and actually see very little of your own agent. If you think you'll want to talk to your agent every day, or at least regularly, the top producers may not be your best choice.

- Education – Educational requirements vary by state. Numerous advanced courses are offered, but the only technical and competence based program available nationwide is the Graduate REALTORS® Institute (GRI) Series, administered under the direction of the National Association of REALTORS®. A REALTOR® who completes the fifteen eight-hour modules and passes subsequent examinations, may then use the designation of GRI.

- Commitment – You must choose someone who is as interested in helping you find the right home as you are.

- Reputation – Check with their local board to see if anyone has filed complaints against them.

- Other factors – There are several other intangibles that you'll want to look out for, too.

GUERRILLA GEEK

Only 15-20 percent of agents have earned the GRI accreditation, but these agents are not difficult to find, since they usually include the designation with their names on business cards and advertisements.

- Knowledge of neighborhood – Be sure you get someone who knows his or her way around and knows the significance of living in one place over another. You would not want an agent that would recommend a particular location, only to find out that the negatives in that particular area outweigh the positives. You'll want someone who can not only be confident about the home they are helping you buy, but also satisfied about the life you will enjoy there after the sale.

GEEKOID

One significant benefit that an agent can offer is access to the MLS, or the Multiple Listing Service. However, most MLS systems now have a community portal that allows anyone access to a portion of the information.

- Personal compatibility – Personalities are an unpredictable factor, but you'll want to get someone with whom you are a good mix. If you are sure of what you want, and don't need a strong outside influence, you will not want a domineering personality to take charge. You will want more of a listener who is willing to accommodate the ideas you already have. On the other hand, if you need someone strong to take you in hand, recognize that and choose accordingly.

- Customer care – Only you know how much personal attention you'll expect during this exciting process. Will you want a follow-up call following each home you are shown? Will you need a call on a regular basis even if there is no news? Know what you will expect, and find out who can give you that so you can agree together about what to expect.

One final consideration before signing with a buyer's agent is whether or not you can cancel your contract if you are unhappy with his or her service. Most reputable firms allow you to cancel (in writing) at any time. However, if you end up buying a home they've shown you, you may still owe them a fee.

 **GEEK AT A GLANCE**

- Once you decide to have a real estate professional help you, you need to know the places to find a good agent, and then know how to select the right agent from among all those available.

- There are numerous places to get the names of qualified agents available to help you, including personal referrals, advertisements, and the Internet.

- Once you have the name of several candidates to help you find a home, interview each one before making your choice.

- Factors to consider when choosing an agent will include their education, knowledge of the neighborhood, experience, commitment to the job, and availability.

- Be sure to find out under what terms you can cancel a contract with an agent before you sign on the dotted line.

TAKING THE GRAND TOUR

Whether you make an appointment to see a home on your own or with the help of an agent, it is exciting to see a home that you might be interested in.

Before you go, here are some suggestions that may be helpful as you begin the exciting, confusing, and yes, fun process of looking at homes.

- Always take another person with you. Not only does this ensure your safety, but it will also offer another set of eyes to look for features you would like, and problems you do not want to take on. Two or more heads really are better than one.

- Carry a notebook with a page assigned to each house you see. Make notes about things you like and dislike to help you as you discuss your choices later. Make a picture of each home to add to the page. Always ask the agent or homeowner for permission first.

- Remember that you are a guest in the home. You don't own it yet. Observe common courtesies like wiping your feet before you enter, keeping your children with you at all times, leaving your food and drink in the car, and putting out your cigarette before you enter.

- Take a tape measure with you to write down critical measurements. If you buy the house, you can always go back and measure for drapes and other custom items, but being able to measure on your first visit might answer some basic space requirement questions.

- See the home at different times of the day. Go during the day and at night. Go in between. There may be traffic, noise, or other problems that occur at a particular time that you may not get to witness with only an occasional visit.

- Don't hesitate to ask for a second visit if needed.

- Don't worry if you miss something. If the deal goes through, you'll want to hire a professional inspector to go over the house in detail to check for problems you should know about.

Taking a Good Look Around

As you arrive at each home for your tour, ask yourself if you could imagine living there. Then, consider the idea more objectively as you look around. Here are some things you may want to think about as you examine the property under consideration.

THE LOT

As you arrive at the property, take note of what kind of first impression it makes. Make sure at some point in the tour to spend some time outside considering these factors:

- Size – If you spend a lot of time outdoors, you'll want a bigger yard to enjoy. If you don't, then something smaller with less maintenance required will be fine.

- Shape – Irregularly shaped lots may not matter to you, but may be harder to sell when you're ready to move on.

GEEK*Speak:*

"No house should ever be on a hill or on anything. It should be of the hill. Belonging to it. Hill and house should live together each the happier for the other."
Frank Lloyd Wright

- Slope – Not only will the slope affect issues like cutting the grass, but it may also affect what you'll be able to add on, or not add, later.

- Drainage – The ability of the soil to absorb water works in conjunction with the slope of the lot to keep water drained away from the home. Low areas that hold water can be a problem inside and outside. You don't want your basement to be flooded (which indicates another problem, too), and you don't want mud holes in your yard, especially near the door. A best case scenario is a slope away from your foundation on all sides. Look for evidence of septic tank problems in the yard as you walk around the property.

GEEK GLOSSARY

Curb appeal is a term that describes how a home looks from the street. The first impression people have of a home is very important to prospective homebuyers.

- Soil – Look for soil that will accommodate a healthy lawn, and even flowers/vegetables if gardening is important. Soil can also affect how a house settles. Of course, if you have any reason at all to think the soil is contaminated, be sure and check that out to allay your fears about potential health issues.

- Hazards – The danger of having high-voltage electrical lines nearby has not been proven, but particularly if you have children, you will not want to take the risk of living near potentially hazardous lines. Look around for these and other possibly threatening elements. Be aware of any offensive odors that may indicate a septic tank or sewage problem.

EXTERIOR

Examine the outside of the house as closely as you do the inside. Be sure to note the following items as you check the exterior:

GUERRILLA GEEK

It's a good idea to visit a potential purchase right after a long rain. That's a great time to check the basement and ceilings for evidence of leaks.

- General state of repair – Note the condition of the exterior, in particular whether it will need repainting in the near future. If so, remember to take that future expense into account when making your offer.

- Roof – The roof is another major part of the home, and if you'll have to replace it soon, that will be a major expense. Make sure you know how old the roof is, and what condition it's in.

- Drains/gutters – Are they in good repair, or are they stuffed with last year's debris? Are they broken and rusted?

- Windows and doors – Make sure doors and windows do not sag and check for broken glass that should be replaced by the seller. Note whether the house includes storm windows or if they'll need to be added.

- Yard – Note not only how the yard has been kept up, but see if there are areas where grass simply won't grow. Will you be left with bald spots?

- Location – Note how close the house is situated to the street. If you have small children or pets, will the location be a problem?

If the property has exterior water spigots, check to be sure they are all frost free or have an interior shut-off valve to prevent freezing.

- Driveway – Is the pavement in good condition, or will it have to be repaired or replaced?

- Walls and fences – Check for the condition of those already in place, and be sure there is room to add any extras needed.

- Surroundings – If there's a rundown building next door, or a convenience store across the street, you may not want to live there no matter how good a deal you're offered.

INTERIOR

As you get the grand tour, try to imagine what it would be like to live in the house. Check especially for these critical items:

- Entrances – Are they convenient and attractive? Do you need a foyer, or would you mind stepping in the front door right into the living room?

- Floor plan – Walk through to note if you are basically pleased with the layout; if you are not, can you remodel to suit your needs, or add on space?

- Major items – Look closely at the air conditioning/heating unit, fuses and circuit breakers, and the appliances. Are they in good shape or will they need to be replaced soon? What about the plumbing?

- Overall condition – Will major repairs to the interior be needed? Will you have to paint either to accommodate personal preferences or to update a worn-out paint job? What is the condition of the floors? Is the carpet stained or worn? Check for evidence of pet stains, which can be hard to remedy short of replacement. Just as you did outside, you'll want to be aware of

GEEKOID

If the home you're touring has an electric water heater, and the area in which it's located is known for hard water, ask if the heater has been cleaned regularly to remove minerals which could shorten the life of the heater.

GUERRILLA GEEK

Ask about the type of paint used on interior walls and trim. Homes built before 1978 may include lead-based paint. Most real estate laws require sellers of homes built before this date to provide a Lead-Based Paint Disclosure to the buyer. For information on the dangers of lead, contact the National Lead Information Center hotline at (800) 532-3394.

any offensive odors that might indicate problems such as leaks or mold.

- Kitchen – Do appliances work? Is there an eat-in kitchen? Do you need features like a double sink, a center island, or extra counter space?

- Cabinet and closets – You will obviously want to note how many there are of each to be sure they can accommodate your storage needs in the kitchen, bathroom, and bedrooms. Be sure to look inside each not just for shelving, but for possible signs of damage that may not be obvious if you look more casually.

- Bathrooms – Make sure all faucets work. Use your ears as well as your eyes—listen for noise while they work. Check grout for cracking or mold. If there are sliding doors around the tub, be sure they work with no problem. Check tracks also for dirt and wear. Look for evidence of leaks where the tub and shower door frame meet. Run water in the sink and flush the toilet to be sure they work, and to note consistency of water pressure.

- Ceilings – Check for evidence of roof leaks or settlement problems. High ceilings look great, but make sure they include a fan or other device to help move air along.

- Closet space – Are closets numerous and spacious enough to meet your needs? Is there supplemental space if closets are limited?

R-values are heat- or cold-resistance values assigned to insulating materials. The higher the R-value, the better the insulation.

- Attic – Check for access to the attic, even if it's only pull-down stairs, and for adequate insulation once you're up there. Inspect ceiling joist, too.

- Laundry space – Is there space and a hook-up for your washer and dryer? Is the laundry area conveniently located? Will you have to carry laundry up and down stairs, or if the laundry room is near the kitchen, will you have dirty clothes on the kitchen floor on wash day?

- Basement – Inspect foundation walls for cracks and spots. Check floor joists that are visible overhead. Check for evidence of termite or mouse droppings that might indicate a pest problem. Look for water stains that might mean occasional flooding.

- Utilities – Ask to see all utility bills for the past year to get an idea of how much it will cost to live there.

AMENITIES

There are certain extras that you may or may not be able to live without. Check those as well. Here are some things that many people look for:

- Vehicle storage space – Make sure it is ample, and is conveniently situated.

- Fireplaces – Many people enjoy the warmth of a fire, but is it a make-or-break item for the family room?

- Pools – Check for repair and maintenance issues.

- Decks and patios – Ask if the deck was made with pressure-treated wood, and if it was not, make sure it is in good shape. Make sure any supports are solid and straight. Check for a secure connection to the house.

GEEKOID

Check to be sure that the deck is firmly connected to the side of the house with bolts. Make sure the bolts and plate are not cracked or rusted.

- Alarms and locks – If you feel the need for these extra measures, check to see if they are already in place, or would need to be added. If the latter is the case, be sure it will be possible.

- Auxillary services – Get information about police and fire coverage, if and how fire dues are paid, and how garbage pick-up is handled. If your child needs bus service to school, is it available?

- Prepare for seeing a home by asking someone else to go with you for a second opinion.

- Take a notebook with you so you can record information about each house you see. Make pictures of them if possible.

- See homes at different times of the day to see if there are problems like traffic or noise that manifest themselves in certain situations.

- Look carefully at each element of a home as you consider it. Divide it into separate units, and be sure to observe components of each part carefully. Major divisions might be the lot, the exterior of the home, the interior, and amenities.

- Remember that you are a guest in the homes you visit, and observe appropriate courtesies.

LET'S MAKE A DEAL

Once you find a house you like, you will need to make an offer in writing. Keep in mind that once you submit it and it is accepted, the document will become a binding sales contract, also known as a purchase agreement.

Because the offer will include terms that you may later have to live with, be sure you spell out what you are willing to do, and not do, as clearly as possible. Here are some items that should be included:

- Address and a legal description of the property

- Price you are willing to pay – No doubt about it, this might be the item you're most interested in. You'll certainly want to give it a great deal of consideration: if you offer too little, you'll likely lose out to

Keep in mind that if you are working solo, i.e., not with a real estate agent, the purchase order or offer you draft must comply with state and local laws. Check to see what requirements apply in your state.

another offer, and if you offer too much, you may be upset later to find out that you could have paid less. Here are some factors that will affect the amount you ultimately offer:

- The asking price of the house – The advertised price of the house is probably not the only price the seller will consider. Even if he or she would like to get the full advertised price, there might be room for compromise depending on how anxious he is to sell.

Be aware before you make an offer that you are signing a legal contract. If the offer is accepted by the seller, you have agreed to buy a home.

- What you can afford – This amount should have been determined earlier in the process. Decide how much cash you have to pay down, how much you can afford each month, and how much you'll need at closing. Then decide if you can pay the asking price, or if you'll offer a different amount.

- Prices for comparable houses – Check the selling prices (not the asking prices) of comparable houses nearby. This will give you an idea of how much to offer for the house under consideration. Most comps will tell the average percent of asking price the neighborhood brings.

- The current real estate market – If houses in the area are in demand for any reason (say, if it's in a great school district), you may not have much luck offering less than the asking

GEEKOID

Comps should be houses that have sold within the last one to six months (so prices are current), should be similar to the one you're interested in, and should be near the home you're considering (to reflect factors related to location).

GUERRILLA GEEK

Some experts recommend that when making an offer in a competitive market, your offer may gain an edge if you write a cover letter to accompany your offer. You could tell the seller about yourself and your family, talk about your desire to live there and why, and what you are willing to do to ensure the sale.

price. But if the current market is sluggish, you may be in the driver's seat. Try to find out how long the house has been for sale. Every month it sits vacant means considerable expense to the seller. He or she may be willing to sell for less for a quick and sure thing.

- The seller's needs – The seller may be interested in a quick sale if he or she has a contract to purchase a new home, or if relocation is in his picture.

- The buyer's needs – There may be something about the house that makes it particularly valuable to you, whereas it might not have that same value to others. For instance, if you have elderly parents that live nearby, you might especially want the house because it's near your parents, and you might be willing to pay more for it than someone else without that factor.

• Terms – Outline how you'll pay—with cash, or will you get a mortgage.

- Seller's promise to provide clear title.

- Target date for closing.

- Amount of earnest money accompanying the offer, and how it will be returned to you if the offer is rejected, or kept as damages if you back out of the deal without a good reason.

- Items that will remain with the property. Anything attached and not specifically excluded stays, but it is still a good idea to restate items you care about. This might include outdoor storage buildings, appliances, window treatments, garage door openers, portable air conditioning units, or decorative items such as chandeliers.

- Items that you want removed such as storage buildings or an old car sitting in the yard.

- Method by which real estate taxes, rents, fuel, water bills, and other utilities are to be adjusted between the buyer and seller.

Earnest money is money that you include with your offer to purchase a house. It shows that your offer is sincere (hence, "earnest"), and assures the seller of your good intentions. The broker or an attorney usually holds the deposit, the amount of which may vary by location. The amount paid will become part of your down payment or closing costs should the sale go through.

GEEK⊙ID

Final walk-throughs are important before closing because they give you one more chance to see the home before you sign for it. See the house after it is vacant to be sure that no damage occurred as the former owners were moving out, and to see that furniture and other items did not conceal major flaws.

- Provisions about who will pay for title insurance, survey, termite inspections, and other incidentals.

- Details about how to handle repairs necessary following inspection.

- Type of deed to be given. The most common is a general warranty deed. Choose how you'll take ownership—as sole ownership or joint ownership with tenancy in common.

- Amount of earnest money and who holds it.

- A provision for a last-minute walk-through before closing.

- A time limit after which the offer will expire.

- Other items required by your specific state.

- Contingencies to the contract – these are possible situations that may affect the sale. When you add contingencies, you are saying that you will only go through with the sale if that event

GUERRILLA GEEK

If you have second thoughts about your offer, you can withdraw it in most cases right up until the moment it is accepted. If you do want to withdraw it, check with a real estate attorney first to learn about your rights. If you withdraw your offer through an agent, be sure you document the time of the conversation. If you can't get in touch with your agent in a timely fashion, you should call the seller's agent directly.

occurs. For instance, if you need to sell a home before you can buy another one, you might make an offer on a house that is contingent on the sale of your current home. Other common contingencies might be the buyer being able to qualify for financing, the home passing certain inspections, or even that the owners be willing to leave all appliances.

GEEKOID

It is infrequent that an initial offer is accepted unless it's full price. Do not be alarmed if your agent indicates that a counter offer has been made.

• Timeline – The seller may want to speed up some parts of the sale, such as the dates for certain inspections.

GUERRILLA GEEK

There are some factors that will make you particularly appealing as a potential buyer, and will put you in a strong bargaining position:

- Offering an all-cash purchase
- Being pre-approved for a mortgage
- Not having a house that has to be sold before you can afford to buy.

Getting a Response from the Seller

Once you or your agent have submitted an offer, you will get some type of response from the seller.

You will receive one of several responses:

- The seller will accept the offer as written.
- The seller will counteroffer.
- The seller will reject the offer.

Let's consider each of those scenarios.

Remember that until you have a signed contract, anyone else can step in and make another offer that may be accepted.

GEEKOID

Buyer's remorse is a feeling common to many homebuyers after they have reached a deal to buy a new home. The enormity of the purchase settles in and creates anxiety because of the responsibility involved. But there are times when concerns are legitimate: if there are problems with the deed, if inspections reveal more problems than you bargained for, you cannot get financing for the home, or if there are property boundary issues that need resolving. Important concerns such as these should be addressed before the sale proceeds.

Acceptance of the Offer. The seller may receive your written offer and sign it just as it stands, unconditionally. If so, it becomes a firm contract as soon as you are notified of acceptance.

Counteroffer. Do not be surprised if you receive a counteroffer in response to your offer. This is the norm. Very few offers are accepted without any change. Common points for counteroffers are the following items:

Gazumping is the term for a seller taking a higher bid from another buyer after he has already agreed to sell to a previous buyer. It comes from the Yiddish word "gazumph," meaning to swindle or overcharge. Believe it or not, this is allowed in the United Kingdom.

- Price – The seller may not be willing to come off the asking price as much as you wanted, but he or she may be willing to compromise without accepting the amount you suggested.

- Closing or occupancy date – The seller may need more time to vacate the property, or may even offer to pay rent and remain after closing if a substantial amount of extra time is needed.

- Contingency of prospective buyer's sale of home – If the seller cannot wait for this to occur, he or she may ask that it be eliminated from the contract.

- Inspections – The seller may want to schedule any inspections earlier than suggested in the offer.

Rejection of the Offer. If the seller rejects the offer, the would-be buyer is free to walk away from the deal without further obligation. Once an offer is rejected or countered, the original offer is dead. The seller cannot later change his or her mind and hold you to the offer. The whole process starts again when the buyer finds another home that he or she would like to buy.

GEEKOID

If the response to your offer is not to your liking, you can make a counter counteroffer. Then the negotiations will continue until an acceptable arrangement is reached, or someone calls an end to the negotiation.

GEEK AT A GLANCE

- Once you find a house, you will make a written offer to buy it.

- Your offer will become a binding contract if it is accepted.

- If you are making an offer without the help of an agent, be sure your offer complies with state and local laws.

- Every element of your intentions should be clearly spelled out. Be sure to include the following items:
  - address of the property
  - price you are willing to pay
  - terms of the sale
  - date for closing
  - contingencies
  - amount of earnest money and who holds it
  - items that will remain
  - items that must be removed
  - particulars about payment of taxes and utilities will be paid/adjusted
  - repairs required and who will pay
  - provision for last-minute walk-through
  - timeline of offer

WHEN THE DEAL GOES THROUGH

Once you and the seller agree on all terms of a sale, you have bought yourself a home. Now here's a whole new list of things you'll need to do.

The first thing you should do after your offer is accepted is to have the home inspected.

Home Inspections

There are three good reasons you should have your potential new home inspected: to evaluate the physical condition; to identify items that need repair, and to estimate the remaining life of major items like your heating and cooling system.

Hire a professional inspector to thoroughly examine all the house's structural systems and give you a

Many states now require sellers to disclose known defects by signing seller disclosure statements. These help protect buyers by giving them support if sellers try to hide problems.

written report outlining any problems found, even small ones. You can find inspectors in the yellow pages, or your agent may have someone he or she regularly uses. This can be beneficial, since they will usually make an appointment sooner than a company you call cold. This inspection will cost about $250, but it's well worth it to turn up any problems you need to know about.

GEEKOID

To be sure that your inspector is current on standards and guidelines, make sure he or she is certified by the American Society of Home Inspectors (ASHI).

Here are some questions to ask an inspector that you are considering for your inspection:

- What is his or her experience?

- What certifications does he or she have?

- How many inspections do they do a year?

- What type of report will you get—written or oral?

- How long will it take?

- What will be included?

GEEKOID

Errors and omissions insurance protects you in the event that there is an "error or omission" in the inspection. Many businesses have this insurance to protect them from the cost of defending themselves if their recommendations or advice are questioned, and to handle the cost of the judgment if they are found to be at fault.

- Does the inspector have errors and omission insurance?

GUERRILLA GEEK

Never skip a home inspection, even if you are buying a new home. New homes are not immune to hidden problems that only a professional can uncover.

Home inspections generally focus on structure, construction, and mechanical systems of the house. They reveal problems that will affect the value of your home, so look at the cost of inspections as an investment. The inspector should issue a written report to indicate repairs that are needed. Here are some items that are typically included:

- Electrical system – Are there code violations that would make living in the house unsafe? Are there smaller problems that you should ask the seller to fix?

- Plumbing and waste disposal – Has the plumbing been properly installed and is it in good working order? Is there any evidence

GEEKOID

The U.S. Environmental Protection Agency and the Surgeon General of the United States have recommended that all houses be tested for radon. For more information, call the National Radon Information Line at 1-800-SOS-Radon or 1-800-767-7236. Ask your real estate agent if radon is a problem in your area.

of leaks? Most inspectors do not inspect septic tanks. This is usually an additional expense if you want a specialist to come out and check the septic tank.

GUERRILLA GEEK

The home inspector does not evaluate the value of the home—only its condition.

- Water heater – Is it in good working order? Is it large enough to handle your needs?

- Insulation and ventilation – Is there adequate insulation in the attic? What about proper ventilation in bathrooms?

- Water source and quality – Are there times when water flow is limited? What about the quality of the water you get?

- Indication of pests – Is there evidence of termite presence that should be treated? What about past damage that should be repaired?

- Foundation – Is the foundation solid, or has it been damaged? Are cracks visible that might indicate structural problems? Is there dampness in crawl spaces or basements?

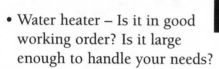

GEEKOID

Be sure to accompany the inspector when he or she checks your home. Not only will it increase the likelihood of seeing all problems that exist, but you can see firsthand what the problems are when you find them.

- Doors – Do uneven doors indicate that the home has shifted?

- Windows – Are there broken windows that should be repaired? Are they efficient for retaining heating and cooling?

The most common environmental toxins for which homes are tested are mold, asbestos, and lead.

- Ceilings – Do ceilings show sign of water damage?

- Walls – Is there damage to drywall that should be repaired?

- Floors – Are floors even and in good shape?

- Roof – Is the roof in good condition, with no leaks? What about gutters?

- Attached structures (sheds, decks, etc) – Are these unsafe or unsightly? Should they be removed?

Other inspections you may want to include are a structural inspection, done by a structural engineer, pool or hot tub inspection, a lead paint inspection, and a radon gas inspection.

GEEKOID

Have your inspector check your chimney, too, for loose bricks, as well as for secure flashing around the bottom to be sure it's watertight.

The Appraisal

The mortgage company will want to have the property appraised to determine how much of a loan they can give you. Some people recommend that this be done first so you don't spend money for inspections on a home that doesn't appraise for the full amount.

An appraiser looks for particular features of a house, whereas an inspector looks for structural soundness.

An appraisal will include a visual inspection, noting approximate age and condition, the number of bathrooms and bedrooms, square footage, lot size, and extras such as garages and porches.

The appraiser will estimate the value for the house, which will be either based on what it would cost to construct a similar home, including land, or by comparing the house to other similar ones in the neighborhood.

Your appraiser will need the following information:

- A plot plan or land survey

- Information on the most recent purchase of the house

- Title, including any easements

- A home inspection report

GUERRILLA GEEK

If you don't agree with the appraised value, you can always contest it.

- Documentation of recent improvements and their costs

The appraisal report will list the address of the property and a description of the neighborhood, including factors like property value trends. It will list features of the house, including particulars such as the number of rooms, materials in each, and floor coverings. It will mention utility systems and even kitchen equipment. It will also present a description of the attic and garage if applicable. It will conclude with descriptions of three comparable properties, an estimate of the value of the home, and a description of how that number was determined.

 *If there is any doubt as to the home's value, do the appraisal first. If it doesn't appraise fully, you won't have wasted money on inspections.*

Pest Control Inspection

Get a pest control company to do a termite inspection, which will cost about $75. The company you get to do a general inspection may also be able to do a termite inspection as well. Besides the fact that a termite inspection is just a good idea, it's also required by your lender.

The termite inspection is a visual inspection of accessible areas of a home for evidence of wood-destroying insects. The inspector will check exterior areas as well as basements and crawl spaces. The attic may also be checked. Findings of the inspection and recommendations

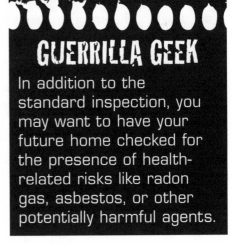

GUERRILLA GEEK

In addition to the standard inspection, you may want to have your future home checked for the presence of health-related risks like radon gas, asbestos, or other potentially harmful agents.

are reported to the buyer and to the mortgage company. The seller probably has a termite bond in place. If so, the bond company will come out and do a wood infestation report, and also any paperwork necessary to transfer the bond.

If termites are found, the problem can be fixed. You'll just have to decide who's going to pay for it. Also, you'll need to specify how it will be done. Some people with children and pets don't want certain chemicals used. Be sure you find a company that can use alternative methods if treatment is necessary.

Septic Tank Inspection and Cleaning

This is usually required if it has not been done within the last twelve months. Even if it is not required by the lender, it is a good idea to include it in the process.

The Survey

Part of the final procedures will be to confirm boundary lines for your property. The mortgage company will naturally want to know exactly where the property they're financing begins and ends. Some mortgage companies simply require a copy of an old survey and a statement from the sellers disclosing that they have not made any

GEEKOID

Not only will you need to know exact property lines for closing the purchase of your house, but if you intend to add a pool, erect a fence, or do any other addition later, you will need to know your boundaries at that time.

changes to the property's footprint since the date of the survey. Unless you see something you want confirmed by a surveyor (such as a fence that may be on the neighbor's property), you can save money by not having a survey.

If your lender does require a survey, it will be done by a professional surveyor to determine whether your property is within property borders, whether there are any easements that could affect title to your property, and if there are any encroachments that should be dealt with.

The report you receive will include a map or drawing of the property showing its precise legal location and other physical features, including any improvements to it. Here are some

If you're having a new home surveyed, chances are that the original surveying pins are still in place, which will make the survey easier, and will cost less as a result.

If the seller has a survey, you may be able to use that survey instead of ordering and paying for a new one.

An **encroachment** is an intrusion upon your property, intentionally or accidentally. An example would be a neighbor's fence built not on the property line, but a couple of feet onto your property. Violations of the property line should be addressed before closing.

other things that the survey will show in addition to your boundaries and encroachments:

- Rights-of-way, easements, and roads – A survey reports all conditions imposed by law. For example, if your local government has a fifteen-foot easement on the back part of your property, you'll want to know up front that it can be taken at any time for municipal use.

The survey will let you know if there are elements of your property that you share with neighbors, such as a driveway or access road.

- Access, ingress, egress – The survey will show if your property has vehicular ingress and egress to an open public street.

- Bodies of water – Nearby ponds and lakes will be indicated on the survey.

- Existing improvements – The surveyer will make sure that any added buildings and other repairs that have been made to the property are in compliance to zoning laws and restrictions, such as specific heights, setbacks, and overall size.

- Telephone, electricity, cables, and water – The report will let you know about the location of underground cables and drains. This will be extremely helpful information if you plan to do additional construction later.

- Zoning classification – There are particular guidelines for what may be built in particular zones. This will define the way(s)

GEEKOID

Because so much of the information on a survey can be helpful in so many ways later, be sure and keep your survey in a safe place. Unlike some of the closing documents, this one can be used later.

that your property can be used. You must know your zone's jurisdiction and classification so you will know for sure what you can and cannot do with your property.

Getting Insurance

You will be required by your mortgage company to have homeowner's insurance for your new property, and you'll have to show proof of insurance at closing. This will protect you against loss from liability, theft, and most common disasters. A standard homeowner's policy will insure both the home and its contents, as well as provide for injuries and property damage that you, your family, or pets might inflict on others. A provision is usually also added to include the cost of living elsewhere if your home is being repaired. Contact a trustworthy insurance agent to decide on a coverage amount that you and your agent are comfortable with. Since many companies offer multi-policy discounts, it is often a good idea to use the same insurance company that handles your car and health insurance, if possible.

There is a formula that the mortgage company uses to calculate how much insurance you are required to obtain. The mortgage company will multiply the replacement value by 80 percent and compare it to your loan amount. The higher of these two amounts will be the minimum required by the lender.

GEEKOID

Don't forget to transfer all utilities to your name at least a week before closing. This should be the last thing you do when you're sure there are no obstacles to closing. Just ask the seller for a list of the utility boards and their phone numbers. They will have to order the services to be turned off before you call and place your order. These may include: electricity, gas, water and sewer, cable, phone, garbage and recycling, alarm monitoring, pest control, and lawn maintenance or service.

A title search and title insurance is also required if you have a mortgage. This ensures that the seller has clear title to convey the property and also protects you from any claims against the property that may arise in the future. Even if you aren't getting a mortgage, a title search is a good idea. If the current or previous owners have any liens against the property, including tax liens, mechanic's liens, or a mortgage, these will have to be satisfied before transferring the deed. Otherwise, you could be stuck clearing these before you can sell the property.

The title search and insurance is typically ordered by the seller's agent or by the closing attorney. However, since this is eventually going to be your policy, you can request that it be handled by your preferred title insurance company. In most states, if the seller has the existing policy paperwork, the company will discount the search fee. Be sure to ask the seller's agent (or your agent) about this discount—a lot of people aren't aware of it.

GUERRILLA GEEK

Once the sale is a sure thing, you should begin changing your address with all banks, credit card companies, and any other accounts you have. You can put a forward order on your mail through the post office, either in person or online at www.usps.com. This will alert you to anyone you forgot when you get mail from them. Don't forget magazine subscriptions, old retirement accounts, and your ISP.

If There Are Problems

If significant problems are found, such as with the foundation or plumbing, your lender might not be willing to go through with the mortgage. But if something smaller is found, you'll need to consider what to do next.

If your contract specifies that the seller will fix all problems, great! The repairs will be made at the seller's expense. If not, you might want to go back to the seller and either ask him to cover the repairs, or lower the price of the house to cover your extra expense.

If you ask for a reduction in price, the seller is not obligated to honor your request. He may figure that the problems were significant enough that you should have noticed them before making an offer. But it can't hurt to ask. He might also feel the same way if you ask him to just pay for all the repairs outright.

An alternative is to ask the seller to pay part or all of your closing costs. The only advantage is psychological. The seller might be so

GEEKOID

If you didn't include in your contract that the seller would pay for necessary repairs, he or she may think you are trying to change the terms of your agreement if you ask for help in making repairs. The seller may be more receptive to this change if you offer several options about how to handle this, such as lowering the sale price or paying closing costs.

insistent on the sale price you've already agreed upon that he's reluctant to change it, but might be willing to make a concession elsewhere.

If all else fails, and the seller won't help you with the extra expense, try to have the repair costs added to your mortgage so you don't have to come up with the cash up front. You should always leave room in your contract to walk away if there are repairs the seller won't make and you don't want to take on.

GEEK*Speak:*

"It is a comfortable feeling to know that you stand on your own ground. Land is about the only thing that can't fly away."
Anthony Trollope

 **GEEK AT A GLANCE**

- No sale of a house should proceed without a thorough home inspection done by a certified and knowledgeable inspector.

- Go with the inspector as he or she looks at the major systems and compartments of the house.

- The buyer should be given a written report which indicates problems found and recommendations for correction.

- A thorough pest inspection should also be performed.

- If significant problems are found, they should be remedied as outlined in the contract. If this was not addressed, negotiations should begin to determine who is willing to pay for what, and if the sale should proceed.

- An appraisal must be done to establish the value of your home, and let the lender know how much they may lend.

- A survey may be required, or a previous survey may be amended, to establish property lines, and to confirm several other important elements of the property.

- Homeowner's insurance is required by the mortgage company to protect the property and its contents, and to insure against damage to others.

- Title insurance is required. Check with your REALTOR® or closing agent with questions about this.

SEALING THE DEAL

Closing is a formal meeting to finalize the sale of the home.

Typically closing is attended by the buyer, the seller, the listing and selling agents, and representatives of the lender and the title company. The closing attorney or title company represents the buyer's mortgage company, not the buyer or the seller.

Basically, the closing process takes the property out of the seller's name and puts it into the buyer's. Once the process is complete, the buyer gets the keys to his new house.

Amid all the excitement, there will be lots of forms to sign. Here are some to be on the lookout for:

- HUD-1 Settlement Statement – This form, required by federal law, itemizes the services provided and lists the charges to the buyer and the seller. Both the buyer and seller must sign it. This is the form you want to look over closely! Make sure all of the figures are correct—they often aren't!

GUERRILLA GEEK

You can ask for a copy of the HUD-1 form the day before closing to give you time to look it over carefully. There may not be time during the closing, although you shouldn't feel pressured to sign before you've had time to look it over.

- Truth-in-Lending (TIL) Statement – This is another document required by federal law. Mortgage lenders are required to give this form to all loan applicants within three business days of receiving their initial application. It discloses the APR, which indicates the cost of the buyer's mortgage as a yearly rate. This rate may be higher than the interest rate stated in your mortgage because the APR includes any points, fees, and other costs.

  The TIL statement also includes other terms of the loan, including the finance charge, the amount financed, and the total payments required.

- The note – The mortgage note represents the buyer's promise to pay the lender according to agreed-upon terms. It presents the date on which payments must be made and the location to which they must be sent. It also details penalties that will be assessed if you default and warns you that the mortgage lender can "call" the loan (require full payment) if you fail to make required payments.

- The mortgage – This is the legal document that secures the note and gives the mortgage lender a claim against the house if you default on the loan. It restates mortgage terms, as well as the responsibilities of the borrower to pay PITI, and to maintain the

GUERRILLA GEEK

During closing, you'll give your Social Security number to the settlement agent. This is to your benefit, since it will allow your tax-deductible interest payments to be reported to the IRS.

GEEKOID

The closing attorney will file your deed and mortgage with your local courthouse. They will either give you a copy of it at closing, or mail you a copy after filing. You have to take this copy to the tax assessor's office to claim homestead on your property. Otherwise, your property taxes may go up (as much as 100 percent) the next time assessment period.

property in general. It also outlines consequences if the borrower defaults on the loan.

- Affidavits – You may be asked to sign numerous affidavits required by state law, the mortgage lender, or by the secondary market agencies. Providing false information may result in criminal penalties, which may include the mortgage lender calling your loan.

- The deed – The seller must bring the deed to the closing, properly signed and notarized, to transfer ownership of the home. You should have already decided what names will appear on the deed, and what type of deed you want (usually a general warranty deed).

GEEKOID

In some states, a "deed of trust" is used instead of a mortgage. Under this arrangement the buyer receives the title to the property, but he or she then conveys it to a third party (a trustee), who keeps the original recorded deed until the loan is paid in full.

GEEKOID

Want to ensure good luck in your new home? According to European tradition, horseshoes hung above doorways will bring good luck to a home. In particular, horseshoes hung in the bedroom will keep nightmares away. The British and Irish versions of this legend insist that the shoes must be turned upward or the luck will "run out."

Among the thick packet you carry away from closing should also be a copy of your HUD-1, appraisal, your survey, any documents pertaining to agents involved in the process, a copy of the purchase contract, and the seller's property disclosure statement.

Getting the Keys

Once all the papers are signed, the checks have been written, and all resolved matters have been settled, you'll be a new homeowner. You'll get the keys to your new house, which is what you came for. Celebrate your hard work and your new acquisition!

GUERRILLA GEEK

Don't forget to check with the seller about additional keys needed, such as keys for a mailbox, or garage door openers. After the closing, you should have all locks changed.

GEEK AT A GLANCE

- Closing is the term used to describe the processing of finalizing the sale of a home.

- Finalizing the sale takes the property out of the seller's name and puts it into the name of the buyer.

- Many important papers will be signed during closing. Make sure to know what each one says.

GEEK GLOSSARY

One of the first things you'll realize when you start to buy a house is that there are all kinds of terms and words you'll have to learn.

You can't learn these all at once, but you can have a good reference on hand for looking up new words and learning them. Here are some you will hear as you try to buy a home.*

A Credit Mortgages - Mortgages which generally meet the credit underwriting guidelines of Fannie Mae, Freddie Mac, FHA, VA, or major jumbo purchasers. Those who have credit ratings or other qualification deficiencies would be rated as B, C, or D credit.

Above Par - When a mortgage is sold for more than its face value because it has an above market interest rate. For example, a $100,000 mortgage may be sold for $101.00, or $101,000.

Acquisition Cost - The sales price of a property plus FHA allowable closing costs. FHA allows certain closing costs to be financed by adding them to the sales price before calculating the required down payment.

Adjustable Rate Mortgage (ARM) - A mortgage in which the interest rate changes at certain intervals during the term of the mortgage.

Adjusted Sales Price - An IRS term for the sales price of a home minus the costs of the sale. Used to calculate capital gains.

* Selected definitions reprinted with permission from *Real Estate By Owner*, "Mortgage Term Glossary," http://www.rbosold.com/mortgage-terms.php.

Adjustment Period - The length of time which dictates interest rate adjustments on an adjustable rate mortgage. A six-month ARM would have an adjustment every six months.

Adjustment Period Cap - The amount that the interest rate is allowed to increase or decrease at the time of adjustment of an adjustable rate mortgage. A one-year adjustable would have an annual cap, since the adjustment period is every year.

Alternative Documentation - Use of bank statements, W-2s, and pay stubs to document an applicant's income and assets instead of verification forms mailed by the lender.

Amortization - When loan payments are made, a portion goes to pay off the principal, and a portion goes to pay off interest. Over time, the interest portion decreases as the loan balance decreases, and more is paid to the principal, so that the loan is paid off (amortized) in the time specified.

Amortization Schedule - A table that shows the principal changes of a mortgage balance on a monthly or annual basis.

Annual Percentage Rate (APR) - Calculation which standardizes rates, points, and other costs of a financing instrument such as a mortgage loan. This figure is disclosed as part of the truth-in-lending statement that is required by the Federal Truth-in-Lending Act. The statement is required on all consumer loans but is required to be disclosed within three working days of application for residential owner-occupied mortgage loans pursuant to the Real Estate Settlement Procedures Act (RESPA).

Application Fee - Fee charged by a lender at the time of loan application. This fee may include the cost of an appraisal, credit report, lock-in fee or other closing costs which are incurred during the process or the fee may be in addition to other charges.

Appraisal - An estimate of value in this case for real property. For residential properties the appraiser would utilize the Uniform Residential Appraisal Report, or URAR. Professional real estate appraisal programs assist the home appraisal process.

Appraiser - An individual qualified to estimate the value of property.

Appreciation - The increase in the value of property over time. This is the opposite of depreciation.

Assumption - The act of taking over the previous borrower's obligation of a mortgage note. Assumptions may be desirable if the terms of the mortgage are advantageous and they are not charged by the lender when the mortgage is assumed.

Back-to-Back Settlement - Transactions involving selling one home and purchasing another on the same day, usually within hours of one another. The seller typically moves from one settlement table to the next in order to accomplish the purchase transaction.

Balloon Mortgage - A mortgage that does not fully amortize over the term of the mortgage. The principal remaining at the end of the term is called a balloon payment.

Base Mortgage Payment - The mortgage amount before financed mortgage insurance or VA funding fee is added.

Bi-Weekly Mortgage - A mortgage that requires one-half of one monthly payment every two weeks. The resulting extra monthly payment each year lowers the mortgage term to approximately twenty-two years from thirty years.

Bridge Loan – Short-term mortgage, usually interest only, utilized to help a purchaser settle on a home before his/her present home is sold.

Broker - Anyone who acts as an agent to bring two parties together for a transaction, and receives a fee for doing so.

Buydown - To lower the interest rate on a mortgage. A permanent buydown would lower the rate for the entire term of the mortgage. A temporary buydown would lower the rate for a certain portion of the mortgage term, usually the first few years.

Capital Gains Income - Income derived through the sale of assets such as real estate.

Capped Rate - A rate commitment by a lender that locks in a maximum rate but allows the borrower to relock if market rates decrease. Also referred to as cap and float.

Cash Out Refinance - A refinance in which the borrower takes cash or equity out of the property.

Certificate of Eligibility (COE) - Certificate issued by VA that gives the amount of entitlement available to a veteran.

Certificate of Insurance - Document that adds the mortgage holder on a particular unit to the master insurance policy for a condominium development.

Certificate of Reasonable Value (CRV) - Appraisal of a property for a VA mortgage. Appraisal of a subdivision would be a Master Certificate of Reasonable Value, or MCRV.

Certificate of Veteran Status - FHA form filled out by the Department of Veteran Affairs in order to establish a borrower's eligibility for an FHA Vet Mortgage.

Clear title - A title that is free of liens or legal questions about ownership of the property.

Closing Costs - The costs incurred in order to purchase real estate. These may include points, taxes, settlement agent fees, and more. They are also called settlement costs.

Co-borrower - Two or more borrowers obtaining the same mortgage. If a co-borrower is not living in the house he/she would be known as non-owner occupant co-borrower.

Combined Loan To Value - The principal balance of all mortgages on the property (including second and third trusts) divided by the value of the property.

Commercial Mortgage - A loan that secures commercial real estate.

Commercial Real Estate - Office buildings, shopping centers, apartment buildings, and other property which is utilized for the production of income rather than as residences. If residential real estate has more than four units it is considered commercial real estate.

Commission - A fee or percentage of the sale allowed to salespeople for handling the transaction.

Commitment - An agreement for future action. A rate commitment would be an agreement to lend at a certain rate. A loan commitment would be an agreement to lend and represent another term for loan approval.

Comparables - Properties utilized in an appraisal to determine the value of the property being appraised.

Compensating Factor - A positive characteristic of a mortgage application which may offset a negative factor.

Compressed Buydown - A temporary buydown that has rate changes every six months as opposed to annually.

Conditional Commitment - Term for an FHA appraisal. An FHA appraisal for a subdivsion would be called a Master Conditional Commitment, or MCC.

Conditional Right to Refinance - A provision of a balloon mortgage that, at the time of the scheduled balloon payment, allows the borrower to convert to a fixed rate for a fixed period, which will fully amortize the mortgage.

Condominium - Multi-unit housing in which each unit owner has title to a unit and has an undivided interest to the common areas.

Condominium Association Fee - A fee paid by the homeowner to the association which governs a condominium complex for his/her part of the maintenance and management of the project.

Conforming Mortgage - A mortgage which can be purchased by Fannie Mae or Freddie Mac.

Construction Mortgage - A loan secured by real estate which is for the purpose of funding the construction of improvements or buildings upon the property.

Construction to Permanent Mortgage - A loan secured by real estate for the purpose of replacing a construction mortgage soon after the improvements are completed.

Consumer Price Index - An index of the federal government's measure of price increases at the retail level.

Contingencies - Conditions that must be met before a contract is legally binding.

Contribution - A cash or other concession by the seller of a property in order to induce a purchaser to buy that property.

Conventional Mortgage - A mortgage not guaranteed by VA or insured by FHA, FMHA, or State Bond Agencies.

Conversion Feature - A feature of a mortgage that allows the conversion to another interest rate, mortgage term, or type of mortgage instrument.

Co-operative (Co-op) - A form of ownership in which the right to occupy the unit is obtained by the purchase of shares in a corporation that owns the building.

Cost of Funds Index - An index showing the cost to depository institutions of acquiring funds.

Coverage - The portion of the mortgage which is insured against default.

Credit History - A record of an individual's repayment of debt. This information is collected by credit bureaus and provided to potential lenders to use in their consideration of loan applications.

Credit Package - The portion of a loan application and documentation comprised of the information regarding the applicant's credit, income, and asset history. The additional aspect of a loan application concerns the property being financed.

Credit Report - A report run by an independent credit agency that verifies certain information concerning an applicant's credit history.

Deed - The legal document conveying title to a property.

Deed of Trust - A legal document which enables the lender or mortgagee to hold legal claim or title to a property while the note is outstanding. The Deed of Trust transfers title to a trustee designated by the lender.

Default - The non-payment of a mortgage or other loan in accordance with the terms as specified in the note.

Delegated Underwriting - The delegation of underwriting authority from an investor or agency to the lender.

Department of Housing and Urban Development - A cabinet level federal agency that houses the Federal Housing Administration (FHA), Government National Mortgage Association (GNMA), and oversight to the Federal National Mortgage Association (Fannie Mae) and Federal Home Loan Mortgage Corporation (Freddie Mac)

Department of Veteran's Affairs - Cabinet level federal agency whose chief purpose is to aid veterans through a variety of programs.

Depreciation - The decrease in worth of an asset over a fixed period of time. This is the opposite of appreciation.

Discount Point - A charge by a lender levied to buy down the interest rate.

Distributive Shares - Increments of FHA insurance from a pool of mortgages insured during the same time period. If over the lifetime of the pool the mortgages perform such that there are shares remaining, they are distributed to the borrowers within that pool. This distribution is currently halted while the FHA insurance fund has been declared financially not sound.

Down Payment - Money given by the purchaser of a property to the seller to acquire the mortgage and hence the property. The difference between the sales price and mortgage amount is the down payment.

Draws - Money taken out of an escrow account in order to finance the rehabilitation of a house. Also refers to increments of money released by a lender as a house is built in the case of construction mortgage.

Earnest money - A deposit paid by a potential buyer to indicate that he or she is serious, or "in earnest" about buying a house or other property.

Easement - A right to utilize property other than one's own. For example, a utility company may be granted an easement for utility lines.

Encroachment - The existence of a protrusion or infringement of a structure on a property.

Equity - The net value of an asset. In the case of real estate, it would be the difference between the present value of the property and the mortgage amount on that property.

Escrow - Money held by a third party on behalf of the first party to be utilized for requirements of a second party. A servicer is a third party that holds an escrow on behalf of a borrower to pay taxes and insurance payments to the applicable entities when they become due.

Exclusive listing - A contract that gives a licensed real estate agent or broker the exclusive right to sell a property for a specified time.

Extended Locks - Mortgage rate commitments which are for longer than the typical sixty day lock-in term.

Fair Market Value - The highest price that a buyer will willingly pay, and the lowest a seller will willingly accept.

Fannie Mae (FNMA) - The Federal National Mortgage Association, the nation's largest supplier of home mortgage funds.

Federal Bond Subsidy Act - Federal legislation empowering state and local governments to issue tax free bonds to fund mortgages for lower and middle income borrowers.

Federal Housing Administration (FHA) - Government agency located within the Department of Housing and Urban Development.

Federal Home Loan Mortgage Corporation (Freddie Mac) - A quasi-governmental agency which is a publicly traded corporation. It was originally chartered by Congress and oversight is located within the Department of Housing and Urban Development. The purpose of the entity is to help facilitate the access of mortgage money by creating a secondary market for conventional mortgages. Conventional mortgages purchased by Freddie Mac are called conforming mortgages.

Federal National Mortgage Association (Fannie Mae) - A quasi-governmental agency which is a publicly traded corporation. It was originally chartered by Congress and oversight is located within the Department of Housing and Urban Development. Conventional mortgages purchased by Fannie Mae are called conforming mortgages.

Fee Simple - Unrestricted ownership of real property.

FHA Direct Endorsement - FHA program in which lenders approve FHA mortgages directly as opposed to submitting the applications to the agency for approval.

FHA Mortgage - A mortgage insured by the Federal Housing Administration (FHA).

Final Inspection - Home inspection made by a lender, VA, FHA, or the appraiser after a new home or repairs have been completed.

First Mortgage - The primary or original loan secured upon real estate.

Fixed Payment Mortgage - A mortgage in which the payment does not change over the term of the mortgage.

Fixed Rate Mortgage - A mortgage in which the interest rate (and usually the payment) does not change over the term of the mortgage.

Fixture - Personal property that becomes real property when permanently attached to real estate.

Float - A loan application in which the lender has not committed to lend at a particular interest rate (the rate is not locked in).

Floor - The lowest interest rate of an adjustable rate mortgage.

Freddie Mac (FHLMC) - An agency of the Department of Housing and Urban Development that creates a secondary market for conventional mortgages.

Free & Clear - A property with no mortgage liability placed upon it.

FSBO - An acronym that stands for For Sale By Owner, as opposed to a home listed for sale through a real estate company.

Full Documentation - Mortgage verification process that relies upon verification forms sent by the lender rather than alternative documentation (such as pay stubs) provided by the applicant.

Fully Amortized - A mortgage that has a zero balance at the end of the mortgage term.

Fully Indexed Accrual Rate - The index plus the margin for an adjustable rate mortgage.

Grace Period - A length of time (usually fifteen days) after a mortgage payment is due, during which the lender will not charge a penalty or report the payment as late.

Graduated Payment Mortgage (GPM) - A mortgage which has regularly scheduled payment increases during some portion of the mortgage term.

Gross Monthly Income - A person's income before deductions for taxes, medical insurance, etc. After deductions, the income is referred to as take home pay or net income.

Ground Rent - The land upon which a home is located is under a long-term lease (leasehold ownership as opposed to fee simple).

Growing Equity Mortgage (GEM) - A type of graduated payment mortgage that has a shorter mortgage term due to future payment increases.

Government Mortgages - Mortgages insured or guaranteed by the government (FHA, VA, FMHA, or State Bond Agencies).

Government National Mortgage Association (GNMA or Ginnie Mae) - Government agency located within the Department of Housing and Urban Development. Created in 1968, its purpose is to facilitate the access of mortgages through creation of a secondary market for government mortgages (FHA and VA).

Grossing Up Income - Income that is not taxed provides more value when qualifying for a mortgage application.

Guaranty - Amount of money VA will reimburse a lender upon default of a VA mortgage. Also referred to as the amount of entitlement or eligibility.

Homeowners' Association Fees (HOA Fees) - A fee typically paid monthly by a homeowner to a homeowners' association in order for the association to take care of areas owned in common by all homeowners within a planned unit development.

Homeowner's Insurance - Insurance carried by the homeowner to protect the dwelling against fire and other hazards.

Index - An indicator that is typically measured by an average of a variable over a certain period of time.

In File Credit Report - Report directly from the credit repositories without any investigative data such as interviews with employers.

Interest Only Mortgages - Mortgage programs that require no repayment of principal. Typical of bridge loans, which will balloon at the end of their term.

Interest Rate Cap - A limit on interest rate increases and/or decreases during each interest rate or over the term of the mortgage.

Investor Purchase - The purchase of a home for the purpose of generating income by renting the property to tenants.

IRS 4506/Request for Copy of Tax Form - IRS Form required by lenders on self-employed loan applications. This form allows the lender to pull tax returns on the borrower directly from the IRS, usually accomplished as a quality control check on a certain number of cases after closing.

Jumbo Mortgage - A mortgage that is larger than the legislated purchase limits of Fannie Mae and Freddie Mac.

K-1 - Federal tax form that reports the income of an individual from a Partnership of Subchapter S Corporation.

Land-to-Value - The value of the land divided by the total value of the property that includes both the land and the home.

Lender Appraisal Processing Program (LAPP) - VA program that allows lenders to directly issue appraisals or CRVs.

Lender Paid Mortgage Insurance - Mortgage insurance program that allows the lender to collect a higher interest rate from the borrower and forward the excess interest to the mortgage insurance company to pay for the mortgage insurance.

Lender Subsidized Buydown - A buydown that has a higher note rate than market.

Leverage - Ability to control a large asset with a smaller asset.

LIBOR Index - London Interbank Offered Rates, the average rate of interest that major London banks are willing to pay each other for U.S. dollar deposits for various terms.

Lien - A claim against a property. A mortgage is one form of a lien.

Life Cap - The amount the interest rate is allowed to increase during the term of the mortgage.

Limited Documentation - Another term for a no income verification mortgage.

Loan-to-Value (LTV) - The principal amount of a mortgage on a property divided by the value of that property.

Lock-in - The process by which a lender commits to lend at a particular rate as long as the mortgage transaction closes within a specified time period. The document that specifies the terms of the lock-in is called a rate commitment or lock-in agreement.

Lock-in Fee - A fee charged by some lenders at the time of lock-in.

Lock-in Period - The period of time for which a lender has guaranteed an interest rate to a borrower.

Lot Mortgage or Lot Loan - A loan secured by real estate that contains no improvements or buildings.

Low/Mod Programs - Acronym for mortgage programs aimed to serve the low-to-moderate income populace.

Margin - The amount added to the index on an adjustable rate mortgage to determine the interest rate at each adjustment.

Master Conditional Commitment (MCC) - An FHA appraisal accomplished for a subdivision.

Mortgage - A loan secured against real estate as opposed to personal property. States that are not trust states utilize a mortgage as the legal instrument to secure the lien against the real estate, which means that the owner holds title rather than a trustee.

Mortgage Insurance - Insurance that protects the lender against default. Insurance can be issued by private sources (private mortgage insurance) or the Federal Housing Administration.

Mortgage Insurance Premium (MIP) - Mortgage insurance charged by FHA to insure a mortgage.

Mortgagee - The lender of money that is secured by real estate.

Mortgagee Clause - Verbiage in the homeowner's and title insurance policies that identifies the mortgage holder and its successors and/or assigns.

Mortgagor - The borrower of money that is secured by real estate.

Negatively Amortized Mortgage - A mortgage whose balance may increase with all or certain payments.

Net Proceeds - Amount of cash that accrues to the seller after expenses are deducted from a home sale.

Non-Conforming Mortgage - A mortgage that cannot be sold to Fannie Mae or Freddie Mac.

No-Income Verification Mortgage - A mortgage that does not verify the income stated by the applicant.

No Point Mortgage - A mortgage that carries a higher interest rate in exchange for no discount points or origination fee.

Note - A legal instrument that specifies the terms of any debt. When someone borrows money secured against real estate, a note will be signed.

Open Equity Line - A second trust mortgage that is an open line of credit. That is, the balance can be increased by future draws up to a set amount.

Operating Income Statement - A form that determines the probable cash flow on a property that is to be used for rental purposes.

Origination Fee - A charge by a lender for the costs of originating a mortgage.

Owner Financing - A property purchase in which the seller provides part or all of the financing.

Owner Occupied Purchase - The purchase of a property for the purpose of the primary residence of the owner.

Partial Entitlement - The entitlement remaining after the veteran has used part of his/her entitlement after obtaining a VA mortgage.

Payment Cap - The limitation on increases or decreases in the payment amount of an adjustable rate mortgage or fixed rate hybrid.

Personal Property - All other property besides real estate (for example, furnishings).

PITI - Total mortgage payment assuming an escrow fund is set up by the lender for real estate taxes and insurance.

Planned Unit Development (PUD) - A project in which there is land and/or facilities owned in common by owners within the development.

Plans and Specs - The plans and specifications upon which the construction of the home is based.

POC - A charge which is paid outside of closing. This would include closing costs such as the appraisal and credit report that an applicant pays up front to the lender.

Point - A charge by the lender. One point is equal to 1 percent of the mortgage amount.

Post Closing Reserves - Liquid assets required by a lender after closing on the mortgage.

Prepaids - Closing costs that are actually paid at closing for charges that will occur in the future.

Pre-qualification - The process of determining one's qualifications for a mortgage and home purchase before the actual home is identified.

Principal - The amount of money borrowed, or the portion that remains unpaid.

Principal Reduction - The reduction in loan balance that occurs with each payment of a positively amortized mortgage.

Private Mortgage Insurance (PMI) - Extra insurance required by lenders for most homeowners who put less than a 20 percent down payment on a home.

Processing - The procedure in which a lender takes a loan application and brings it to the point of underwriting for loan approval.

Profit and Loss Statement (P&L) - A financial statement provided by the applicant who reports the income and expenses for a business during a certain time period.

Purchase Money Mortgage - A mortgage obtained to finance the purchase of real estate.

Qualification - The process that determines whether an applicant can be approved for a mortgage.

Rate Reduction Refinance - The refinance of an existing mortgage balance solely to lower the interest rate.

Ratio Method - Method of qualifying which divides the monthly mortgage payment by the gross monthly income of the borrower and then divides the monthly mortgage payment and monthly debt payments by the gross monthly income.

Real Estate Settlement Procedures Act - Federal law which regulates the settlement practice and the real estate industry.

Real Estate Taxes - Local government taxes levied on the ownership of real estate.

Real Property - The ownership of real estate.

Recapture Tax - A federal tax required on the gain from the sale of certain properties financed under the Federal Bond Subsidy Act which are sold within ten years of purchase.

Recordation Fees - Fees charged by a local government to record the documents of a real estate transaction.

Recorder - The public official who keeps records of transactions that affect property in the area.

Reduced Closing Cost Mortgage - A mortgage which carries a higher interest rate in exchange for no points and/or a credit towards other closing costs from the lender.

Refinance Mortgage - Money borrowed by the present owner of real estate to replace an existing loan secured by the same real estate or to place a mortgage on free and clear property.

Rehabilitate - The process of reconstructing or improving property which is in a state of disrepair.

Rental Equivalency - A mortgage payment after the tax deductions are taken into consideration.

Rental Negative - The monthly cash flow loss on an investment property.

Residential Mortgage - A loan which is secured by residential real estate.

Residential Real Estate - Housing built and owned for the purpose of a person making the property his/her home or a property to be rented to tenants.

Residual Method - Method of qualifying which subtracts all expenses from a borrower's income to determine whether a positive residual remains.

Reverse Annuity Mortgage - A mortgage which uses present equity in the property to fund monthly payments from the lender to the borrower in lieu of the borrower receiving the proceeds of the loan in a lump sum.

Revolving Credit - Open lines of credit which are subject to variable payments in accordance with the balance.

Right of First Refusal - A provision that requires the property owner to give a party the first opportunity to purchase or lease a particular property before it is offered for sale or lease to others.

Right of Recission - A period of three full days after closing in which the consumer is allowed to negate an owner occupied refinance transaction.

Right of Survivorship - The right of survivors to acquire the interest of a deceased joint tenant.

Right to Financial Privacy Act - Places restrictions upon governmental authorities having access to copies of the financial records of any mortgage applicant.

Roll-in - To include the closing costs of a refinance transaction in the balance of the mortgage.

Sales Concession - Something a seller pays of value to a purchaser in order to entice the purchaser to buy the home.

Scheduled Negative Amortization - A mortgage which has planned increases in the balance of the mortgage during some portion of the mortgage term.

Second Home Purchase - A property purchased for occupancy by the owner but which will not be the primary residence.

Second Mortgage - A loan which is secured by real estate already secured by another loan referred to as the first mortgage.

Second Trust - Another term for a second mortgage.

Secondary Market - A market that exists for the purchase and sale of mortgages and servicing rights as commodities.

Self-employment - A person who owns at least 25 percent of the entity that generates income for that person.

Servicing - The process by which a lender collects monthly mortgage payments and forwards applicable portions of the payments to the investor, local government, and insurance agencies.

Settlement - Another term for closing.

Settlement Agent - A person or entity that coordinates or conducts a closing or settlement.

Shared Appreciation Mortgage - A mortgage that offers the lender the ability to realize future gains based upon future appreciation of the property, in exchange for a below market interest rate.

Sole Proprietorship - A form of self-employment in which the individual that is self-employed has formed no separate legal entity such as a corporation.

Staff Appraiser - An appraiser who works as an employee for a mortgage company as opposed to the company hiring an independent firm to appraise properties.

Streamline - A rate reduction refinance that requires less documentation than full package mortgage applications.

Subsidize - A term for aid. Federally subsidized mortgages typically have an interest rate lower than market because of government assistance.

Survey - The measurement of the boundaries of a parcel of land, including any improvements, easements, or encroachments within the boundaries of the property.

Take Back - When the seller uses the equity in the property to provide a mortgage for the purposes of financing the purchase for the buyer.

Take Home Pay - One's paycheck after taxes and other deductions have been subtracted.

Tax Deduction - An expense that the government allows you to subtract from your income before the tax liability is computed.

Tax Service Contract - A service performed by a tax service company that identifies the payment due date of local taxes for the servicer.

Teaser Rate - A starting rate that is below the fully indexed accrual rate (FIAR) on an adjustable rate mortgage.

Temporary Buydown - A lower interest rate on a mortgage for a fixed period at the beginning of the mortgage term.

Term - The period or life over which a mortgage exists.

Title - Ownership record of the property.

Title Company - A company that specializes in examining and insuring real estate titles.

Title Search - A check of title records to confirm the legal owner of property and to ensure that there are no liens or other claims against it.

Transfer Taxes - Taxes levied by a state or local government upon the transfer of real property.

Transmittal Form - A form that summarizes the date contained within a loan application.

Treasury Constant Maturities Indices - A series of indices issued by the federal government that measure the yield of treasury securities for the term measured by the index.

Truth-In-Lending Act - Federal law that requires a truth-in-lending statement to be disclosed for consumer loans. This statement would include disclosure of the annual percentage rate, or APR, as well as other facets of the mortgage program.

Underwrite - The process by which a lender analyzes risk.

Uniform Residential Appraisal Report - The appraisal form which is utilized by appraisers of residential properties to be financed with FHA, VA, and conventional mortgages.

Uniform Residential Loan Application Form - A form accepted by all major mortgage sources for application of residential mortgages.

Uniform Settlement Statement - Settlement summary form required by RESPA to be used by closing agents.

Variable Income - An income form that will vary from year to year.

Verification of Deposit - A form that verifies an applicant's liquid assets held with a particular financial institution.

Verification of Employment - A form that verifies an applicant's job history, including employment date, salary, year to date income, income for the past year, and probability of continued employment.

Verification of Mortgage - A form that verifies an applicant's mortgage history with a financial institution, including the date of the mortgage, present balance, present payment, and history of late payments.

Veterans Administration (VA) - An agency of the federal government that guarantees residential mortgages to eligible veterans of military service.

W-2 - IRS form that reports income taxes withheld by an employer from a particular employee during a calendar year.

W-4 - IRS form that determines the amount of federal taxes the employer will withhold from a person's paycheck each pay period.

Worked Up - Process by which a fully verified loan application is prepared by the processor for underwriting.

INDEX

A

A-frame homes, 82
Accredited Buyer Representative
 (ABR), 102
Adjustable rate mortgages
 (ARMs), 76-78
Affiliated business relationship
 disclosure, 54
Agencies, real estate, 108-110
Agents, real estate, 97-117
 Desirable qualities of,
  113-117
 How to find, 111-113
 Virtual, 108
American Society of Home
 Inspectors (ASHI), 140
Amenities, 127-128
Annual Credit Report Request
 Service, 24
Application fee, 35
Appraisal, 144-145
Appraisal fee, 35
Attorney fee, 36

B

Balloon notes, 77
Bankruptcies, 18, 26-27
Banks, 40-41
Bonds, 16

Bounced checks, 28
Buyer's agent, 104-107
Buyer's remorse, 136

C

Cape Cod home, 82
CDs, 16
Checking accounts, 15
Closing, 35-37, 155-159
Colonial home, 82-83
Comparable Market Analysis
 (CMA), 101, 103-104, 107
Condominiums, 64, 79, 85-87
Consumer Credit Protection Act,
 51
Contingencies, 133-134
Conventional loans, 71-74
Co-operatives, 79, 88
Cosigner, 29
Cottage, 82
Credit cards, 28-29
Credit report 15, 51, 52
 Content, 26-27
 Getting a copy, 24-25
 Inaccuracies, 27
 Inquiries, 25, 27
Credit report fee, 35, 47
Credit score, 21-30, 61
 Improving, 27-29
 Requirements 63, 70, 73

Credit unions, 41
Curb appeal, 121

D

Debt-to-income ratios, 17, 63, 70, 73
Deciding to buy, 9-13
Deed, 157
Department of Veterans Affairs, 64
Disability insurance, 18
Document prep fee, 36
Dual agencies, 109

E

Earnest money, 132
Employment history, 16, 26
Encroachment, 147
Equifax, 21, 25
Exclusive Buyer Agent (EBA), 102
Experian, 21, 25
Exterior home features, 122-123

F

Fair Credit Reporting Act, 24
Fair Isaac and Company, 22
Fannie Mae, 71-72
Fee simple homes, 79-86
FICO® score, 22-23
FHA loans, 61-64
Fixed mortgage rates, 75
Flood certification fee, 36

For Sale By Owner (FSBO), 99
Foreclosure, 18
Freddie Mac, 71-72

G

Garden home, 82
Gazumping, 136
GI Bill of Rights, 68
Good Faith Estimate, 42-43, 53
Graduate REALTOR® Institute (GRI), 115

H

Homes
    Types of 79-89
    Visiting, 119-128
Home inspections, 139-144
Home owner's insurance, 55-56
HUD-1 Settlement Statement, 36, 155

I

IRAs, 15
Inspections, 141-149
    Home, 139-143
    Pest control, 145-146
    Septic tank, 146
    Survey, 146-149
    Toxins, 145
Insurance, 149-151
Interest-only mortgages, 77

Interest rate caps, 76
Interior home features, 124-127

J

Jumbo loans, 72-74

L

Lead-Based Paint Disclosure, 125
Lender's inspection fee, 35
Listing agent, 101-104
Loan discount fee, *See* Points
Loan origination fee, 35
Loan to value, 65
Lock-in agreement, 54-55
Lock-in rate, 55
Lots, 120-122

M

Making an offer, 129-138
Money markets, 15
Mortgages, 39-43, 51-59, 61-78,
    156-157
    Applying for 51-59
    Rates, 75-78
    Terms, 74-75
    Types of, 61-74
Mortgage broker fee, 35
Mortgage brokers, 42
Mortgage companies, 39-40
Mortgage insurance premium
    (MIP), 63, 65, 70, 73

Multiple Listing Service (MLS),
    97, 103, 116

N

National Lead Information Center,
    125
National Radon Information Line,
    143
Notary fees, 36
Note, 156

O

Open house, 107
Overall caps, 76

P

Patio home. *See* Garden home
Pay stubs, 15
Periodic caps, 76
Pest control inspections, 145-146
Planned Unit Development
    (PUD), 80
Points, 35, 53
Prepaids, 36-37
Pre-approval, 37, 46-48, 52
Pre-qualification, 37, 45-46, 52
Principal, Interest, Taxes, and
    Insurance (PITI), 63, 70,
    72-73
Private Mortgage Insurance (PMI),
    33, 65, 74

Processing fee, 35
Profit and Loss statement, 15

R

Ranch homes, 81
REALTORS®, 99-100
Recording fees, 36
Row house, 85

S

72 hour docs, 53
Savings accounts, 15
Savings and loan associations, 41
Self-employment, 15-16
Septic tank inspections, 146
Serviceman's Readjustment Act,
    See GI Bill of Rights
Single agencies, 108-109
Single-family homes, 64, 81-87
Social Security number, 16, 26,
    156
Split foyer, 83-84
Split level home, 83
Stocks, 16
Subagencies, 108
Sub-prime, 71
Survey, 36, 146-149

T

Tax liens, 27
Tax related service fee, 35

Tax returns, 15
Termite inspection, 36,145-146
Title insurance, 36, 150
Title search, 150
Total Debt Service Ratio (TDSR),
    56
Town house, 84-85
TransUnion, 21, 25
Transaction brokers, 109
Truth in Lending Act, 51
Truth-in-Lending (TIL) Statement,
    156

U

Underwriting fee, 35
U.S. Environmental Protection
    Agency, 141

V

VA loans, 64-70

W

W-2, 15, 54
Walk-throughs, 133
Wire transfer fee, 35

Z

Zoning, 92-93